Strengthening Financial Management

Dale F. Campbell, *Editor*

NEW DIRECTIONS FOR COMMUNITY COLLEGES

ARTHUR M. COHEN, *Editor-in-Chief*
FLORENCE B. BRAWER, *Associate Editor*

Number 50, June 1985

Paperback sourcebooks in
The Jossey-Bass Higher Education Series

Jossey-Bass Inc., Publishers
San Francisco • London

EDUCATIONAL RESOURCES INFORMATION CENTER

Clearinghouse For Junior Colleges

UNIVERSITY OF CALIFORNIA, LOS ANGELES

Dale F. Campbell (Ed.).
Strengthening Financial Management.
New Directions for Community Colleges, no. 50.
Volume XIII, number 2.
San Francisco: Jossey-Bass, 1985.

New Directions for Community Colleges
Arthur M. Cohen, *Editor-in-Chief;* Florence B. Brawer, *Associate Editor*

New Directions for Community Colleges (publication number USPS 121-710) is
published quarterly by Jossey-Bass Inc., Publishers, San Francisco, CA 94104, in
association with the ERIC Clearinghouse for Junior Colleges. *New Directions* is
numbered sequentially—please order extra copies by sequential number. The
volume and issue numbers above are included for the convenience of libraries.
Second class postage rates paid at San Francisco, California, and at additional
mailing offices.

The material in this publication was prepared pursuant to a contract with the
National Institute of Education, U.S. Department of Education. Contractors
undertaking such projects under government sponsorship are encouraged to express
freely their judgment in professional and technical matters. Prior to publication,
the manuscript was submitted to the Center for the Study of Community Colleges
for critical review and determination of professional competence. This publication
has met such standards. Points of view or opinions, however, do not necessarily
represent the official view or opinions of the Center for the Study of Community
Colleges or the National Institute of Education.

Correspondence:
Subscriptions, single-issue orders, change of address notices, undelivered copies, and
other correspondence should be sent to Subscriptions, Jossey-Bass Inc., Publishers,
433 California Street, San Francisco, California 94104.

Editorial correspondence should be sent to the Editor-in-Chief, Arthur M. Cohen, at
the ERIC Clearinghouse for Junior Colleges, University of California, Los Angeles,
California 900024.

Library of Congress Catalog Card Number 84-82367

International Standard Serial Number ISSN 0194-3081

International Standard Book Number ISBN 87589-740-1

Cover art by WILLI BAUM

Manufactured in the United States of America

This publication was prepared with funding from the National Institute of
Education, U.S. Department of Education, under contract no. 400-83-0030.
The opinions expressed in the report do not necessarily reflect the positions
or policies of NIE or the Department.

Ordering Information

The paperback sourcebooks listed below are published quarterly and can be ordered either by subscription or single-copy.

Subscriptions cost $40.00 per year for institutions, agencies, and libraries. Individuals can subscribe at the special rate of $25.00 per year *if payment is by personal check*. (Note that the full rate of $35.00 applies if payment is by institutional check, even if the subscription is designated for an individual.) Standing orders are accepted.

Single copies are available at $8.95 when payment accompanies order, and *all single-copy orders under $25.00 must include payment*. (California, New Jersey, New York, and Washington, D.C., residents please include appropriate sales tax.) For billed orders, cost per copy is $8.95 plus postage and handling. (Prices subject to change without notice.)

Bulk orders (ten or more copies) of any individual sourcebook are available at the following discounted prices: 10–49 copies, $8.05 each; 50–100 copies, $7.15 each; over 100 copies, *inquire*. Sales tax and postage and handling charges apply as for single copy orders.

To ensure correct and prompt delivery, all orders must give either the *name of an individual* or an *official purchase order number*. Please submit your order as follows:

Subscriptions: specify series and year subscription is to begin.
Single Copies: specify sourcebook code (such as, CC1) and first two words of title.

Mail orders for United States and Possessions, Latin America, Canada, Japan, Australia, and New Zealand to:
Jossey-Bass Inc., Publishers
433 California Street
San Francisco, California 94104

Mail orders for all other parts of the world to:
Jossey-Bass Limited
28 Banner Street
London EC1Y 8QE

New Directions for Community Colleges Series
Arthur M. Cohen, *Editor-in-Chief*
Florence B. Brawer, *Associate Editor*

CC1 *Toward a Professional Faculty*, Arthur M. Cohen
CC2 *Meeting the Financial Crisis*, John Lombardi
CC3 *Understanding Diverse Students*, Dorothy M. Knoell
CC4 *Updating Occupational Education*, Norman C. Harris

Contents

Foreword

To strengthen the financial management of our colleges and universities, we must do more than merely shepherd resources; we must utilize these resources to implement educational values and meet institutional goals. This considerable task falls most often on the shoulders of chief business officers. A certain degree of schizophrenia is virtually a prerequisite for their job. Business officers must be comfortable with both mortarboards and pin-striped suits, with issues of educational quality and the demands of bottom-line management. Yet this ability to straddle two worlds effectively is also, perhaps, their chief asset. On a daily basis they must negotiate between the worlds of learning and finance; they must keep the long-range mission and goals of their institution in mind even as they work to secure the financial underpinnings that permit its continued existence.

Stereotypes have long distorted the role of business officers and the considerable talents that many bring to their jobs. Caricatures of unfeeling bureaucrats crunching numbers are just as out of date as those of starry-eyed academics having little understanding of institutional reality. Interestingly enough, these misperceptions can be traced, in part, to a period of rapid growth and prosperity in higher education. When the fiscal pie grew larger and sweeter with every passing year, business officers were all too often regarded as functionaries who served up increasingly generous portions. Questions of values and educational effectiveness were left to administrators, trustees, and academics who felt little need to look closely at the books or at the changing world around them. As this period of growth turned to one of retrenchment and decline, business officers encountered the mirror image of this caricature; they were seen as callous administrators who threw out the pie knife only to replace it with fiscal hatchet.

Fortunately, these misperceptions are being corrected. There is now growing recognition that we cannot seek simple solutions to complex bottom-line problems, nor can we see these problems in isolation from educational values and institutional goals. This latest volume in the *New Directions for Community Colleges* series comes, then, at an opportune time. The contributions in this book encourage us to reconsider and articulate the important role of business officers in strengthening financial management and thereby securing educational excellence.

Quite appropriately, this volume casts a wide net; in today's educational and business world, the responsibilities of college business officers now extend to new and different domains. Nevertheless, some common lessons emerge. Scrupulous management of resources and knowledgeable budgeting, accounting, and personnel management are absolutely necessary, but they are not in themselves sufficient. Business officers must aim not only for efficiency but also for effectiveness; they must not only ensure that the institution is doing things right but also that it is doing the right things. This requires that they establish and maintain a strong and clear sense of organizational identity—and that they make major decisions on the basis of that identity. Budgeting, programmatic, and enrollment policies must all reflect an institution's mission and goals. This does not suggest that administrators lose touch with the environment but rather that they aggressively seize the opportunities it offers to support creative and effective educational programs.

To carry out this important charge, business officers must become full partners and team members in all policy decisions affecting institutional and educational effectiveness. Surely none of us can afford to let fiscal responsibilities narrow educational vision nor allow the tyranny of the bottom line to compromise imagination.

Ben Lawrence
C. A. Roberson

Ben Lawrence is president of the National Center for Higher Education Management Systems in Boulder, Colorado.

C. A. Roberson is founding president of the National Council of Community College Business Officials and is executive vice-chancellor of Tarrant County Junior College District in Fort Worth, Texas.

Editor's Notes

The financial constraints of this era continue to influence community college leaders to seek new ways to do more with less and to find new sources of revenue. Adaptive strategies are being sought that are not only changing the organizational structure of community colleges but also the roles and styles of the leadership of these institutions. The chief business officer's or CBOs role has become increasingly important as trustees look to their managerial ability to meet the "bottom line" of any necessary budget cuts (Campbell, 1984).

Few fiscal officers actually relish, during these periods of decline, their reputation as Mr. or Ms. No, even though budget control is inherent in their roles. For instance, Calver (1984), reporting on his nationwide study of community college CBOs, found that the current function these officers identify as most important and that they personally perform (rather than delegate) is the administration of the budget. Until recently, Kaludis (1984) reports, the CBO's role has always been focused on functions where management and control were the exclusive domain (by default) of the business officer.

In today's complex world of institutional management, "leadership" has become the battle cry, and the underlying assumption is that, through strategic management and vision, colleges can create alternatives and attain their preferred futures. Peck (1984) states that this shift in chief executive style is necessitating an accompanying shift in the role of the CBO to become part of the entrepreneurial team. Recent research by Chaffee (1984) on successful turnaround management strategies of declining colleges tends to support Peck's view. She found that successful schools were led by people who sought to construct reality in accordance with their perceptions of what the organization ought to be, that there was a shared perception of what the college was about, and that it was capable of making good on its promises.

Ben Lawrence, speaking to the inaugural conference of the National Council of Community College Business Officials, urged business officers to look beyond the bottom line. Lawrence (1984) stated that "business officers should regard it as a primary task to find the money to support creative programs. Efficient business management yields dollars. But effective programs and effective external communications are the best strategies for acquiring substantial new revenues—invest in them" (p. 23).

Each chapter in this volume examines new strategies to strengthen financial management from the perspective of community college finance and administrative support officers and the changing roles of their positions. The National Council of Community College Business Officials, an affiliate of the American Association of Community and Junior Colleges, and the National Center for Higher Education Management Systems have cooperated in assembling authors with an operational perspective for this sourcebook.

The first section focuses on selected role functions that CBOs now perform or in which they share responsibility. In Chaper One, Byron N. McClenney and Ellen Earle Chaffee ask whether or not the budget implements the important values of the institution. They propose a model for the readers' consideration that has been successful in integrating academic planning and budgeting in both periods of institutional growth and decline. In Chapter Two, Ann L. Kaneklides reviews various cost-accounting models that can provide the basis for an effective management tool for decision makers. In Chapter Three, Harold L. Throop, Jr., reaffirms some basic principles in purchasing and maintenance to further enhance the cost-effectiveness of these programs. In Chapter Four, David R. Bauske proposes new sources of student financial aid as community colleges face reductions in federal sources.

The second section focuses on the shift in community college leadership toward working as an entrepreneurial team. In Chapter Five, John T. Blong and Adelbert J. Purga focus on the importance of institutional research and review environmental scanning methods for enhancing sound financial planning. In Chapter Six, Wayne J. Stumph examines the future of auxiliary enterprises and contracting as colleges increasingly view these services as potential new sources of revenue. In Chapter Seven, Bernard J. Luskin and Ida K. Warren provide a smorgasbord of new strategies that institutions can utilize in generating new financial resources. In Chapter Eight, Charles E. Taylor, Jr. and Dennis Greenway share the importance of an institution possessing an effective investment policy to maximize their returns once they have raised those additional resources.

The third section concludes the volume by looking at emerging issues and implications for strengthening the financial management of community colleges. In Chapter Nine, Richard L. Alfred examines fourteen emerging public policy conditions that will require the attention of financial administrators between 1985 and 1990. He calls for the professional development of the business officials in public policy analysis to enhance their capacity for strategic management of their respective institutions. In Chapter Ten, I synthesize the implications for the emerging role of the CBO, the impact on the organization, and the need for further research. Finally, in Chapter Eleven, Jim Palmer and Diane Zwemer review the literature on strengthening financial management in the community college.

As dwindling resources have made finance an increasingly important topic at community colleges, there has been an unfortunate tendency to emphasize financial management as the end rather than the means to an end. Even though the strategies shared in this volume are focused on finance, they are dedicated to enhancing excellence in teaching and learning in our institutions.

Dale F. Campbell
Editor

References

Calver, R. A. "The Role and Functions of the Chief Business Officers in Community Colleges." Paper presented at the National Council of Community College Business Officials' conference, Dallas, Texas, November 1, 1984.

Campbell, D. F. "Business Officials Contribute Much to Excellence." *Community and Junior College Journal,* 1984, *54* (5), 7.

Chaffee, E. E. "Successful Strategic Management in Small Private Colleges."*Journal of Higher Education,* 1984, *55* (2), 212–241.

Kaludis, G. "The New Improved Business Officer." *Business Officer,* 1984, *18* (3), 29–32.

Lawrence, B. "Beyond the Bottom Line." *Community and Junior College Journal,* 1984, *54* (5), 21–23.

Peck, R. D. "The Entrepreneurial Business Officer." *Business Officer,* 1984, *18* (4), 31–34.

Dale F. Campbell is an assistant professor and the coordinator of the community college education program at North Carolina State University, Raleigh, as well as the executive director of the National Council of Community College Business Officials, headquartered at the university.

Part 1.
Management Functions

Does the budget implement the important institutional values? Effective college management depends on the answer to this question.

Integrating Academic Planning and Budgeting

Byron N. McClenney
Ellen Earle Chaffee

Leading an institution to reexamine its purposes and to set high standards is an act of will on the part of a leader. In fact, what may be missing in all the current talk about leadership, quality, and excellence is an essential ingredient for individual leaders and their organizations. The missing ingredient is the will to decide—the willingness to dream dreams and take risks for the benefit of the organization. Since the only constant in our society may be change, it is imperative for leaders to be proactive rather than reactive, optimistic rather than pessimistic, and to seek to order or control events rather than to be simply a victim of events. Nothing less will suffice in an era of shrinking resources, intense scrutiny, and conflicting expectations.

The Big Question: Does the Budget Implement the Important Values?

Institutional responses to today's challenges will have a greater impact if those responses demonstrate a clear sense of purpose or

D. Campbell (Ed.). *Strengthening Financial Management.* New Directions for
Community Colleges, no. 50. San Francisco: Jossey-Bass, June 1985.

direction. A look at how a college allocates its resources, for example, easily reveals whether the institution leads an "examined" life. The budget should reflect the institution's examination of the difference between what is and what ought to be. In fact, the budget should reflect the values of the organization, and it should reveal choices about future directions for the institution.

Defining or reaffirming the core values underlying college operations is a significant first step for an institution concerned with making the best use of its resources. If resources such as money, people, space, and time are allocated in a manner that reinforces the most important values, then the college strengthens its ability to cope with conflicting expectations or declining resources. Commonly, institutions find it useful to develop statements of philosophy and purpose or mission and to involve faculty and staff in discussions leading to common understandings.

Clarity regarding the core values then provides a basis for developing a collective vision about what the institution should become as it responds to needs in a particular service area. This collective vision provides a strong link between planning and budgeting. In other words, if a department head understands the core values and shares the collective vision, then he or she is more likely to make decisions supporting the mission of the college.

Stating and restating a vision of the institution's potential in the face of rapid change is, then, an essential function of college leaders. An interactive, collegewide process that involves diverse individuals in the definition of this vision ensures that the resulting goals are realistic and that those who will be responsible for carrying them out have been involved in formulating them (McClenney, 1980).

The Institution: Developing or Deteriorating?

The goal orientation just described is a crucial ingredient if institutions are to remain healthy organizations. This sense of what is important can drive an organization to be a developing institution even in the face of shrinking enrollments, shrinking resources, or both (Millett, 1977). In fact, the institution makes the choice as to whether decline means deterioration or not.

Institutional leaders must decide that it is important to clarify and/or reaffirm organizational purposes and then be willing to take the risks inherent in holding discussions about these purposes. Special-interest groups, for example, surface quickly when there is a perceived threat to the comfortable way of conducting business.

Similarly, it may be difficult to define the conditions that should exist when an organization is at its best. Failure to set the directions, however, is to decide to let the college drift and decay. Failure to set high standards is to decide to settle for something less than the best in seeking to fulfill the purposes of the organization. But, given clarity of purpose, leaders can seek the involvement of all who are a part of the enterprise in moving toward desirable outcomes (Bean and Kuh, 1984). Choosing an effective and efficient process through which to plan and allocate resources is crucial.

An institution must decide to plan and then must develop a systematic chronology that ensures that one phase of budgeting is completed before its results are needed for another phase (Armijo and others, 1980; Kieft, Armijo, and Bucklew, 1978; Van Ausdle, 1980a and 1980b). In addition, when everyone knows the chronology of events, they can participate more fully and appropriately. The approach selected should take into account the following elements:

1. There should be a simple format and a definite schedule.
2. There should be a way to look beyond the bounds of next year.
3. The process should be simple and call for brief periods of intense activity.
4. The process should be directly linked to institutional decision making.
5. Planning should be viewed as a prerequisite to the allocation or reallocation of resources.
6. Stress must be placed on an ongoing process of internal and external assessment.

The Task: Identification of Critical Issues

Given the choices to affirm important values and to be a developing institution, a college must assess the realities within which it must operate. The identification of critical issues provides a base of useful information for all parties involved in the planning process.

Among the important external realities to assess are demographics, political realities, economic realities, social forces, and the impact of technology. Significant in the internal environment may be the results of program reviews, facility utilization, collective bargaining, the organizational structure, the impact of tenure, affirmative action, and resource allocation.

The realistic identification of constraints and opportunities often can be achieved best by a representative planning group or planning council. Since it is important to focus decision-making efforts on critical issues, and since the credibility of the people translating data into useful information is crucial, the choice to use a representative group can ensure acceptance of its conclusions (Keller, 1983).

Out of the assessment activity should flow information for strategic decisions and guidance for operational planning (Shirley and Volkwein, 1978). In order to focus the efforts of the organization on those areas that have the most to do with the health of the institution, the planning council might categorize the information in two ways:

1. Planning assumptions—These statements identify the trends, constraints, and opportunities facing the institution.

2. Planning guidelines—These statements reflect decisions made to guide planners at all levels in the institution. With these two sets of information, the planning council is in a good position to recommend action priorities for the next year in the life of the organization.

An annual cycle of activity through which an institution can create or update a strategic plan (which includes decisions about future directions), develop an operational plan for the year ahead, and allocate or reallocate resources is the most desirable structure. All of these activities can be driven by decisions made as a result of examining the critical issues facing the institution. Position papers can facilitate the decision making that flows out of the assessment we have described here.

A Case Study

Many of the essential elements in the model presented above are illustrated in the planning and budgeting process used at Stanford University during the 1970s (Chaffee, 1983). Under the leadership of Provost William F. Miller and Vice-Provost Raymond F. Bacchetti, the process for allocating resources changed from what might be called a poker model, with one dealer and a host of players, to a systems model. A dozen or more leaders in both academic and business administration in the university interacted among themselves and with a variety of committees and faculty representatives in mutually understood and complex ways to support commonly held goals.

Early in the decade, Provost Miller stated his budget objectives. He planned to achieve an equilibrium between the growth rates of income and expense. He also planned to apply four criteria in assessing budget requests: academic importance, excellence or the potential for excellence, student interest, and funding potential. The most important features of these objectives are that they expressed the core values of the university and that Provost Miller used them, explained his budget decisions in terms of them, and held to them for many years with unswerving determination. The goals were so ambitious that they could not be achieved in a year or two, but, by implementing them gradually and consistently, the university was able to make recognizable progress in the directions Miller intended.

The university protocol was a major tool in the effort. The protocol was a systematic way of eliciting desired information from all relevant actors in the budget process. It began with a letter from Miller to the deans in which he outlined the major factors that were expected to influence plans and budgets for the following year. Then he identified his priorities and concerns and invited the deans to submit their budget requests. Before these requests became written documents, however, Miller met with each dean individually to discuss them. Miller stated in his protocol letter that he expected his discussions with the deans to (a) relate budget decisions to the university's program goals, (b) stimulate critical analyses of existing structures and functions, (c) compare actual performance with prior plans, and (d) increasingly relate budgeting to planning.

Simultaneously, the academic and financial planning staffs met to define the financial parameters of the budget. They ran several iterations of the computer program that modeled their five-year financial situation, the Long-Range Financial Forecast. Each version incorporated refined assumptions and data as information about costs and revenues, garnered from diverse sources both inside and outside the university, became available. A similar exercise, limited to the coming year, made use of more detailed information to estimate the necessary budget parameters that would meet the decision makers' overall criteria for an acceptable budget. When these exercises were complete, the provost knew how much was available in each broad category of expense and what trade-offs he might be able to make without sacrificing financial well-being.

Inevitably, requests exceeded available resources. But, as Bacchetti (1978) often stated, " 'We haven't enough money' is an unacceptable response to a request. We have lots of money. The question is, 'Is this item high enough on the priority list to be funded?' " The requests were arrayed into a list called the Migration Analysis, as candidates for various kinds of funds, from operating budget funds to restricted or grant funds to no funding. How much of

Figure 1. Chronology and Steps in Budget Decisions

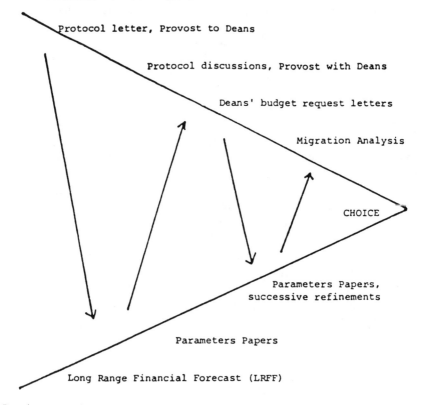

Selecting Among Competing Claims

Protocol letter, Provost to Deans

Protocol discussions, Provost with Deans

Deans' budget request letters

Migration Analysis

CHOICE

Parameters Papers,
successive refinements

Parameters Papers

Long Range Financial Forecast (LRFF)

Setting Overall Budget Parameters

September   February

Source: Bacchetti, 1978.

the request's cost went into each funding column was determined
largely by how well the request met the provost's funding criteria. The
iterative nature of the process is illustrated in Figure 1. The
September-to-February timeline correctly suggests that the activity
level is very high during that period and rather relaxed at other times.

The entire planning and budgeting cycle is illustrated in Figure
2. Although space does not permit reviewing the entire cycle here, one

Figure 2. The Annual Operating Budget Cycle

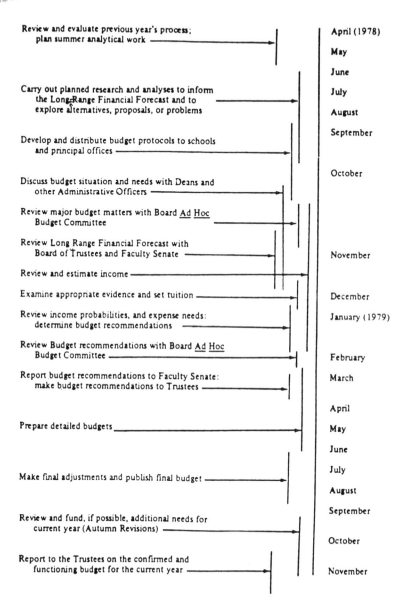

Review and evaluate previous year's process; plan summer analytical work ⟶	April (1978)
	May
	June
Carry out planned research and analyses to inform the Long-Range Financial Forecast and to explore alternatives, proposals, or problems ⟶	July
	August
Develop and distribute budget protocols to schools and principal offices ⟶	September
Discuss budget situation and needs with Deans and other Administrative Officers ⟶	October
Review major budget matters with Board Ad Hoc Budget Committee ⟶	
Review Long Range Financial Forecast with Board of Trustees and Faculty Senate ⟶	November
Review and estimate income ⟶	
Examine appropriate evidence and set tuition ⟶	December
Review income probabilities, and expense needs: determine budget recommendations ⟶	January (1979)
Review Budget recommendations with Board Ad Hoc Budget Committee ⟶	February
Report budget recommendations to Faculty Senate: make budget recommendations to Trustees ⟶	March
	April
Prepare detailed budgets ⟶	May
	June
Make final adjustments and publish final budget ⟶	July
	August
Review and fund, if possible, additional needs for current year (Autumn Revisions) ⟶	September
	October
Report to the Trustees on the confirmed and functioning budget for the current year ⟶	November

Source: Stanford University, 1979, p.14.

aspect of it is especially noteworthy. Figure 2 was included in a widely available publication by Stanford University (1979) called *Operating Budget Guidelines* (OBG) every year for ten years. So one key feature of the Stanford process is its consistency, its predictability. Those who wished to affect planning or budgeting outcomes could easily determine how and when to get involved. Another key feature is the fact that the vice-provost wrote, published, and distributed the OBG year after year. Anyone, on campus or off, who wanted one could have it. This measure, too, served to make the process accessible to all.

In summary, the Stanford case illustrates several principles recommended in this chapter. It points out how core values can be used effectively in planning and budgeting as decision criteria. It shows a highly interactive, iterative process that is nevertheless orderly and predictable. The process was clearly and firmly guided by explicit assumptions and priorities. It fostered both a wide array of good ideas and a cohesive consolidation of the best of those ideas. Finally, the process used routine analytical formats, regular schedules, brief intense activity, and simultaneous consideration of alternatives. The consensus at Stanford is that it worked very well.

Of course, such planning activities are not limited to four-year colleges and universities. Another example (Moore, 1983) illustrating the flow of activity in an annual cycle can be found in the process utilized in the Alamo Community College District (Texas). The cycle is initiated in early January as a representative planning council comes together to examine all available assessment information for the purpose of updating the strategic plan and the creation of assumptions, guidelines, and priorities for operational planning. As illustrated in Figure 3, the process culminates in the development of a budget for the next fiscal year.

The Outcome: Wise Decision Making

Most leaders would like to think they engage in rational decision making as they face the many choices that arise throughout the life of an institution. Even under the best of circumstances, however, most would acknowledge the collegial, political, and bureaucratic concerns impact efforts to make rational decisions (Chaffee, 1983). Given those realities, leaders need to cultivate an atmosphere in which core values and shared goals can influence decision processes. They also need to recognize the interaction in a complex organization of several other methods of making decisions, such as:

Figure 3. The Budgeting/Planning Process at a Community College

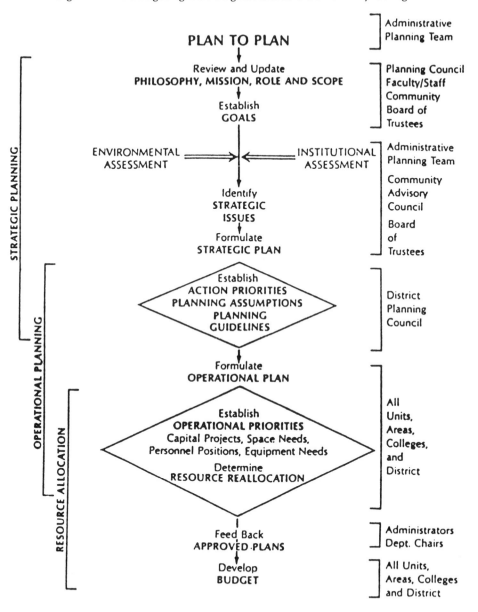

Source: Moore, 1983.

1. Collegial processes—These assume shared responsibility among peers who reason together toward their common goals. Solutions emerge that reflect consensus or at least satisfy most of the actors. The time required for this process can be excessive.

2. Political processes—These recognize the diverse interests among units of the organization. A forum is provided in which differences are worked out. Negotiation marks the process, and the fittest survive or get the most resources.

3. Bureaucratic processes—Systematic procedures mark these processes, which focus on operational efficiency. Incremental budgeting in many institutions may provide the most concrete example of the process.

4. Organized anarchy—Diversity of goals and scarcity of time and other resources tend to produce this process. Choices are almost accidental, and ambiguity permeates the organization.

Wise leaders realize the importance of the pattern of interaction, and they structure processes to tap the strength inherent in that interaction. They also recognize competing interests and seek to facilitate consensus building within the organization. Further, they should demonstrate the interdependence necessary for an institution charged with implementing a purpose or mission. Unifying people for the good of the institution should certainly be a primary objective as leaders develop an approach to decision making.

Planning and budgeting as envisioned here are at the heart of decision making for the institution. Budgets are going to be developed regardless of planning, and it is important to realize that an emphasis on costs and short-term interests has dominated the decision-making processes of most institutions in the past. Thus, institutions that want to exercise some control over their futures will need to make a conscious effort to ensure that planning becomes more effective and apparent in their budgets (Caruthers and Orwig, 1979; Dickmeyer, 1982). What is needed is a situation in which strategic planning guides operational planning and operational planning guides the allocation and reallocation of resources. What is needed is a routine in the annual life of the organization to update strategic plans, develop operational plans, and to allocate resources in line with the critical choices made as a college considers its alternatives for the future. What is needed is a stream of wise decisions based on an understanding of the external environment in which the institution operates and the honest assessment of internal strengths and limitations (Cope, 1981).

The Linkage: Planning and Allocation of Resources

Institutional leaders should anticipate certain barriers when trying to link planning and the allocation of resources. Among the most frequently observed are: fear of change; lack of time to plan; protection of "turf"; bad attitudes based on previous planning efforts; collective bargaining; competition; lack of commitment; lack of skills in establishing priorities; declining resources; and apathy. Alertness to these potential barriers is crucial as an institution addresses the major priorities in effective planning and budgeting. In addition to clarity and commitment regarding philosophy, mission, goals, and assessment, the institution should give attention to the following:

1. The strategic elements, such as philosophy, mission, goals, assumptions, guidelines, and action priorities, provide guidance and direction for planning by all units of the institution. These elements are developed or updated as a result of assessment activity.

2. A representative planning council or task force should be convened on an annual basis to examine the critical issues facing the institution. They should review completed studies and develop or update the strategic plan. They should develop the planning assumptions and guidelines for planning at all levels of the organization.

3. All units should be involved in developing the plans they will implement. Guided by the assumptions, guidelines, and action priorities that the planning council has developed, units should use an interactive process to address the following:

- A summary of achievements or results for the current year, which can serve as an evaluation of whether or not a unit did what it said it would do
- A statement of desirable outcomes for the next year, developed in line with the strategic decisions made about the future
- A set of projections for the second year in a cycle of activity, based on the assumption that plans for the next year can be completed
- A staffing and financial summary, updated to reflect the major implications of the desirable outcomes.

Through consolidation of the unit plans within each of the various areas (such as instruction, student services, and business services), it is possible to develop priorities for personnel, capital equipment, and capital projects for each area. The group process of consolidation certainly involves elements of collegial, political, bureaucratic, and rational decision making. The intended outcome of agreement on priorities for funding can be achieved without regard for the amount of money available. What is important is for college leaders to struggle with choices based on plans.

Once area plans are developed, a repetition of the consolidation effort can produce a plan for the institution. Through utilization of a specified format, severe page limitations, and intense activity during brief periods of time, it is possible to involve all units of an organization in a healthy process that does not become "paper oriented." The consolidation of plans forces people to select the most important information for inclusion, and discussion of priorities for funding leads to an easier time during line-item budgeting.

The Strategy: Involvement

Every leader of a functional unit (such as a department) should feel a responsibility to help the institution fulfill the potential described in the strategic plans. He or she should be expected to involve the faculty and staff members of the unit in the development of a unit plan that describes the contribution of the unit. He or she should expect to be involved with peers in the development of an area plan in which priorities for future funding are identified. This involvement will be boosted if there is clarity regarding the core values and the collective vision of the institution. As indicated earlier, when everyone knows the chronology of events, all leaders can participate more fully and appropriately. For example, a unit workshop might be held on March 1, followed by an intense three-week work period. Once the unit plan is complete, the unit leader would be involved in a work session on the area plan. He or she would then wait for feedback before proceeding to develop budget requests for the next fiscal year.

If priorities for use of personnel and acquisition of equipment are dealt with during the review of plans, then the matter of developing a line-item budget becomes simple since more than 85 percent of the budget is set. Communication is facilitated by work at the unit and area levels. Consensus building is possible because people have the opportunity to review plans developed by others under the guidance provided by the planning assumptions, planning guidelines, and action priorities. If there is conflict between competing interests, then at least there is a structure through which to work. Consensus is the target, but decisions can be made, if necessary, even without consensus because all the plans are on the table at the same time. The energy of the organization can be focused on the future with specific action steps providing the bridge to the allocation of resources.

References

Armijo, F., and others. *Comprehensive Institutional Planning: Studies in Implementation.* Boulder, Colo.: National Center for Higher Education Management Systems, 1980.

Bacchetti, R. F. Academic Planning Office Seminar, Stanford University, Stanford, Calif., 1978.

Bean, J. P., and Kuh, G. D. "A Typology of Planning Problems." *Journal of Higher Education,* 1984, *55,* 35–55.

Caruthers, J. K., and Orwig, M. *Budgeting in Higher Education.* Research Report no. 3. Washington, D.C.: AAHE-ERIC, 1979.

Chaffee, E. E. *Rational Decision Making in Higher Education.* Boulder, Colo.: National Center for Higher Education Management Systems, 1983.

Cope, R. G. *Strategic Planning, Management, and Decision Making.* Washington, D.C.: American Association of Higher Education, 1981.

Dickmeyer, N. "Financial Management and Strategic Planning." In C. Frances (Ed.), *Successful Responses to Financial Difficulty.* New Directions for Higher Education, no. 38. San Francisco: Jossey-Bass, 1982.

Keller, G. *Academic Strategy: The Management Revolution in American Higher Education.* Baltimore, Md.: Johns Hopkins University Press, 1983.

Kieft, R. N., Armijo, F., and Bucklew, N. S. *A Handbook for Institutional Academic and Program Planning: From Idea to Implementation.* Boulder, Colo.: National Center for Higher Education Management Systems, 1978.

McClenney, B. N. *Management for Productivity.* Washington, D.C.: American Association of Community and Junior Colleges, 1980.

Millett, J. D. (Ed.). *Managing Turbulence and Change.* New Directions for Higher Education, no. 19. San Francisco: Jossey-Bass, 1977.

Moore, K. M. "An Integrative Process for Strategic Planning, Operational Planning, and Resource Allocation in a Multicollege Community College District." Unpublished doctoral dissertation, University of Texas at Austin, 1983.

Shirley, R. C., and Volkwein, J. F. "Establishing Academic Program Priorities." *Journal of Higher Education,* 1978, *49,* 472–488.

Stanford University. "Operating Budget Guidelines, 1979–80." Stanford, California: Stanford University, 1979.

Van Ausdle, S. *Comprehensive Institutional Planning in Two-Year Colleges, Vol. I: An Overview and Conceptual Framework.* Columbus, Ohio: National Center for Research in Vocational Education, 1980a.

Van Ausdle, S. *Comprehensive Institutional Planning in Two-Year Colleges, Vol. II: A Planning Process and Case Study.* Columbus, Ohio: National Center for Research in Vocational Education, 1980b.

Byron N. McClenney is chancellor of the Alamo Community College District in San Antonio, Texas.

Ellen Earle Chaffee is director of the Organizational Studies Division of the National Center for Higher Education Management Systems in Boulder, Colorado.

When community college administrators know how to use cost information and analysis properly, the value of such information to the decision-making process is greatly enhanced. Accurate accounting information provides an effective management tool but cannot act as a substitute for good management.

Cost Accounting for Decision Makers

Ann L. Kaneklides

In community colleges throughout the United States, the design of cost accounting and information systems has become a major concern of chief business officers, top executive management, and the various funding sources of these institutions. Due to revolutionary changes in student population and declining economic governmental resources, administrators are more sensitive than ever to the importance of accurate cost reporting for use in planning and control. In cost-accounting systems, costs are accumulated primarily to enable managers to predict accurately the financial consequences of alternative decisions. It is this facet of effective management information systems that will be vital to community college leadership and management throughout the next decade: informed decision making through accurate anticipation of cost incurrence in light of changing economic and environmental conditions. Development of causal relationships between institutional management decisions and cost incurrence is essential to this process. In any event, community college administrators must be able to discern the data relevant to a particular decision. "Different costs for different purposes" provide the valid information needed for sound decisions.

D. Campbell (Ed.). *Strengthening Financial Management.* New Directions for Community Colleges, no. 50. San Francisco: Jossey-Bass, June 1985.

Cost Accounting: What It Is and What It Does

Scheps and Davidson (1978) note that Milesell and Hay's (1961, p. 619) *Governmental Accounting* defines cost accounting for governmental agencies as "that form of accounting activity which is designed to furnish information concerning the cost of units of services or goods produced. To a large extent, governmental expenditure accounting and statements have been confined to recording and reporting how much was spent; unit cost accounting, on the other hand, is an endeavor to record, measure, and report how much was accomplished and at what price" (p. 282).

However, with the rapidly increasing use of cost-accounting systems by both businesses and government agencies, this definition has broadened considerably. Cost accounting now incorporates the gathering and supplying of information for all types of decision-making needs, from daily operations management to nonroutine strategic decision making and major organizational policy formulation. The primary purpose of cost accounting is to enable management to make decisions, with the simultaneous examination of alternative decision studies and the implementation process. When management evaluates various accounting techniques and information systems, however, the most important criterion is whether a particular alternative motivates behavior in these decision and implementation processes that is in agreement with overall top management goals.

Accounting systems used to accumulate data for decision making must be designed, then, with a focus on predetermined top management objectives. An important question to ask is, "How does an accounting technique or system affect the managers who provide data input for the system and the overall organization?" It is critical that the effects of an information system on motivation and decision making be scrutinized and considered. In other words, does the information system designate objectives and motivate actions that agree with overall organizational goals made at the strategic planning level?

In addition to the motivational aspects of an information system, management should consider the purpose of the system. A valid information system retrieves data closest to where they originate, then processes and transforms those data into a form useful to the decision makers. However, many institutional administrators and managers, as well as managers of commercial entities, have been turning to the cost-accounting or information system for *decisions* instead of useful *data*. The information delivery process should not be mistaken for the decision-making process. Cost accounting cannot be a substitute for effective management practices (Ameiss and Kargas, 1981). Because criteria for decisions should be instituted by those responsible for results, operating managers and administrators must take responsibility for seeing that the proposed system can answer questions in light of the decisions management must make. An effective cost system promotes the decision-making process by providing data to answer such questions as "What are the costs of changes in course scheduling and course offerings?" or "What should it cost to add another academic program?" It traces the operating costs of the organization to its products or services, and it compares actual and budgeted performance to identify variances for timely reporting.

Experienced accountants have never professed to be able to compute exact costs, especially the full costs of a product or service. They have also recognized that some cost measurements may be lacking in accuracy. Therefore, administrators must recognize that no cost measurement should be viewed singly, such as an efficiency variance, at the expense of another one just as important in evaluating performance.

Fundamentally, there are three essentials for implementing a cost-accounting system effectively: user training, user participation in system design and implementation, and top administration and management support of the system. Inadequate communication and the inability to use the data provided by the system in a proper manner are the most detrimental influences on implementation.

When ascertaining the kinds of cost data that are needed for a particular cost analysis, management should remember the purpose for the information collection, who will utilize the cost information, and the information level needed to satisfy the users. As the cost of implementing any information system may be substantial, the potential benefits of data collection must be weighed against the corresponding costs. Before any cost studies are performed, management should evaluate the accuracy and adequacy of historical and current accounting data. If present accounting data are inaccurate, it would be more advantageous to the institution to overhaul its present system than to spend additional resources on complex cost studies.

What About Full Allocation of Costs?

The cost-accounting system that most accurately gauges causal relationships is probably the system that will produce data leading to the best decision making. However, systems that show the full allocation of costs, including indirect or overhead costs, are often defended on the premise that they remind management that support of the whole institution is important for a department or program to operate well, even though causal relationships may not be clearly identified. Because service departments facilitate the offering of curriculum programs in a community college, no program (or product) cost should be relieved of an equitable share of these support costs. Service department costs are every bit as much a part of the program (or product) costs as are faculty salaries and supplies (or direct labor and direct materials). In full costing, all institutional costs are funneled to the product (such as a curriculum).

Accountants or managers who advocate full allocation of costs regardless of substantiated causal relationships indicate that harm due to cost overstatement is less than that due to the understatement of costs (management will not be as prone to overexpand, for example). Costs allocated to programs or departments regardless of controllability may help management understand the benefits offered by other departments, as well as the costs incurred by those departments. Many who argue for full allocation of costs assume that managers usually don't care whether these overhead costs are allocated, as long as all departments are subject to the same cost-allocation methods. However, this is advantageous only to the extent that there is no resentment about allocation procedures among administrators or managers and that it prompts no misunderstanding of information in cost studies. For budgetary control reasons, controllable and uncontrollable costs included in the same report should be identified separately. Regardless of the method of cost allocation chosen, special consideration must be given to its effect on management behavior.

Looking for Causal Relationships

Among the most controversial aspects of a cost-accounting system in almost any organization is the allocation of indirect costs to products and services. While the determination of an allocation base is necessary because there is no direct connection between the cost object and the incurred cost, this determination is dependent on the reason for the allocation, the cost object, and the total cost. The best allocation base assists in predicting fluctuations in total costs, and in showing continuing relationships in cost behavior patterns. Various guides exist to help those designing a cost system to arrive at an allocation base reflecting causal relationships. Among these guides are the observability of physical relationships, the specification of cost relationships through a knowledge of organizational operations, and the identification of relationships through regression analysis. However, if there appears to be no logically defensible base, no allocation should be made, or the costs should be allocated by prior agreement, with all data users understanding the arbitrary nature of the allocation.

Many times costs are traced to departments or responsibility points. However, this allocation of costs seldom stops at the location of individual management responsibility. Responsibility accounting, while extremely important for evaluating performance, does not relate costs specifically to a product (such as a curriculum program). After costs have been traced to responsibility points, it is often necessary to further allocate these costs to construct decision alternatives. This may be difficult when service departments are in question. For example, the community college maintenance department may originate costs on behalf of other institutional programs. These costs may be allocated to various programs or departments as a cost of maintaining a specific curriculum or program.

Before choosing among various allocation bases, however, administrators must determine cost behavior patterns because failure to ascertain these patterns may result in an inaccurate cost analysis. Whether a cost is fixed, variable, or mixed affects the choice of an allocation base.

In *Costing for Policy Analysis,* the National Association of College and University Business Officers (1980) suggests the systematic application of a cost behavior analysis procedure to specify or approximate cost behavior patterns. Community college administrators and managers should first ascertain policy questions and the management level that will utilize the data for decision making. Second, factors influencing those costs, such as the activity or activity measures, need to be determined. Then, for each chosen activity, management must identify present levels of service and the related costs, and the subsequent cost behaviors of each activity. Finally, top management or administration must assess the policy implications of the cost analysis. It would also be extremely helpful to administrators to document the manner in which the analysis results can influence future policies.

Selecting an Allocation Base

When choosing an allocation base, the institution may consider criteria such as services used, facilities provided, physical identification, or benefits received. While the services-used criterion is usually a clear matter of cost incurrence, such as repairs, many times there is no breakdown of the fixed and variable components of these costs. Where fixed costs are significant, this may lead to imprecise presuppositions of causal relationships. If separate allocation rates are utilized, these differences in causal relationships will be taken into account. Fixed costs of a service department may be based on a previously agreed-upon sum for furnishing the fundamental ability to serve, while variable costs might be allocated on the basis of services used. On a monthly basis, a predetermined sum to allocate costs to departments or programs and a predetermined standard unit rate may be used to allocate variable costs. Fixed costs should be allocated according to the decisions bringing about the fixed commitments. In other words, what factors determine the equipping of the service department?

Because costs are usually incurred through a decision on the part of the cost object, the allocation base ideally should have some physical connection with that cost object. Substantial confirmation of causal relationships is generally rendered through physical identification.

The benefits-received criterion is usually not considered as acceptable as the three other criteria mentioned. It is based on the presumption that indirect (overhead) costs should be allocated to departments or products based on the relative benefits received by these departments or products (Horngren, 1972).

College administrators and other users of data generated by the information system should be cautious of the full allocation of service department costs when those support costs are allocated on the basis of actual hours used in servicing other departments or programs, and the rate exercised is formulated by dividing the total costs incurred in the support departments by the total hours used by other departments or programs. The sums charged to the other departments or programs may be subject to determinants not under the control of the heads of those departments or programs, such as the efficiency or quality of services rendered by the support department, or the unit price. Also, a particular time period's charges to one program or department are subject to how much of the support department's service was being utilized by other departments or programs.

Bases are generally selected after management has weighed the costs needed to apply the allocation base and other apparent factors already associated with the product. Another important consideration is whether there would be any differences in the final outcome among the various allocation bases. If only small differences arise, administrators may prefer the easiest method of allocation. Cost information may be compiled into "pools" in a number of different ways: by fixed or variable costs, by responsibility points, or by function. The allocation base is applied to the cost pool because the cost of performing a more detailed cost allocation would be more than the advantages received.

Community college administrators and business officers may find the application of one rate for variable costs and another rate for fixed costs more appropriate for their information needs, as it allows for a cost breakdown in cost-volume analysis during the decision-making process. Also, two rates promote the merging of information systems for both budget control and department or program costs.

Figure 1 describes various allocation bases and can assist college administrators and business officers in choosing the method most compatible with their information needs.

Allocating Indirect Costs

The "direct method" of allocating overhead costs ignores services rendered by one service department to another and allocates overhead costs directly to the other producing departments or curriculum programs. It is based on the assumption that the support provided by all service departments contributes directly only to the product costs (such as program costs). The "step-down method" of allocating overhead costs recognizes support given by one service department to other service departments. The cost-allocation progression starts with the service department that gives support to the largest number of other service departments, and it continues through the allocation of costs of the service department that furnishes support to the fewest number of departments. However, after a support department's costs have been allocated, no subsequent support department's costs are reallocated back to it.

Hyatt (1983) outlines a general five-step cost-accounting procedure to assist college administrators in the collection of cost data:

1. *Determine specific cost objectives and cost centers.* Use a standard chart of accounts to separate institutional functions into different cost objectives or cost centers. Cost centers may refer to activities, such as printing, or to function, such as general administrative services.

2. *Choose consistent categories of cost.* The organization's classification of expenditures by object should serve as the foundation of the cost categories. Expenditure breakdowns are dependent on the needs of the decision makers.

Figure 1. Possible Allocation Bases

SUPPORT SERVICES/ ACTIVITIES	Actual Usage: -job orders -purchase orders -service requests -voucher count	Total Direct Costs	Assign. Sq.Ft.	Total Comp.	Instr./ Res./ Public Serv. Comp.	Stu. Head-Counts	Total Hours of Use	Stu. Credit Hours
STUDENT SERVICES: Student Services Admin.		X						X
Social & Cultural Activ.		X				X		X
Counseling & Guidance		X				X	X	X
Financial Aid Admin.	X				X			X
Student Admissions & Records	X				X			X
Health & Infirmary Services		X			X		X	
INSTITUTIONAL SUPPORT: Executive Management		X		X				
Fiscal Operations	X	X		X				
General Admin. Serv.	X	X		X				
Logistical Services	X	X						
Community Relations		X					X	
PLANT OPERATION & MAINTENANCE: Physical Plant Admin.	X	X	X					
Building & Equipment Maintenance	X	X	X					
Custodial Services	X	X	X					
Utilities	X	X	X					
Landscape & Grounds Maintenance	X	X	X					
Major Repairs & Renovations	X	X	X					
ACADEMIC SUPPORT: Course & Curriculum Development		X			X			
Academic Computing	X	X						
Audiovisual Services	X				X			
Academic Administration & Personnel Development	X	X						
Libraries	X	X			X		X	X

Source: Hyatt, 1983, p. 19.

3. *Assign tier-one costs to cost centers or objectives.* Tier-one costs are direct costs that can be identified easily with a particular cost center. For instance, in the student services area, financial aid administration's tier-one costs would include staff salaries, materials and supplies, and so on.

4. *Assign all tiers two and three costs to specific cost objectives and cost centers.* Tier-two costs are those costs that include all tier-one costs *and* indirect costs reflecting the value of support services furnished to other cost centers or cost objectives. Tier-three costs include tier-two costs *and* depreciation or use charges on plant and equipment.

5. *Develop output measures.* The analysis of data is the last step. Sometimes other statistical data may be combined with cost data to calculate unit costs. Comparative analysis of costs over various time periods may assist administrators in evaluating efficiency.

What About Depreciation?

An element of cost that is most important to cost studies and data compilation for community colleges is depreciation. However, colleges are the only nonprofit institutions that are prohibited from charging depreciation in the Statement of Current Funds, Revenues, and Other Changes. The 1973 American Institute of Certified Public Accountants (AICPA) *Audit Guide for Colleges and Universities* was issued with the advice of the National Association of College and University Business Officers (NACUBO), which indicates that the audit guide meets user needs. This treatment of depreciation is at variance with generally accepted accounting principles for profit-oriented organizations and with the audit guides of other nonprofit entities. Carl Ebey (1982) notes that the 1975 Price Waterhouse "Position Paper on College and University Reporting" addresses the subject of depreciation:

> While relatively few colleges follow depreciation accounting techniques, we believe financial statements of colleges should reflect the cost of operations for the period so that trustees can better judge financial results. Buildings and equipment wear out, and if one is trying to measure costs, the cost "expiration" or depreciation must be considered (pp. 13–14).

As depreciation is a cost to the institution, this cost should be recognized when performing cost analyses of educational programs, regardless of current financial reporting requirements.

Implications for the Community College

The growing emphasis on accountability to the public the community college serves and to college's funding sources necessitates that these institutions address the need for a cost-accounting model for use in various decision-making processes, such as planning, control, performance evaluation, budgeting, and other areas. Cost information is one factor in the formulation of a method in which the institution can attain its long-term mission goals. Examining the cost requirements of each decision alternative allows administrators to utilize available resources more effectively, and possibly to alter the budget plan to coincide with changing economic priorities.

Cost data for current operations control assists managers in identifying areas in which corrective actions must be taken, and it involves a comparison of actual costs to budgeted costs for assistance in the determination of areas in which adjustments may be required in future planning and budgeting. In addition to assessing the effectiveness of educational activities, the process of evaluation encompasses an analysis of present funding levels to ascertain whether particular activities should be intensified, reduced, or eliminated. Cost data are vital to the process of evaluation for funding purposes, tuition price setting, interdepartmental charges, and charges for student housing, among many others.

Cost information is being used more than ever for internal management and control in community colleges—and for external reporting to state legislatures and local governments as the focus on cost-based funding formulas to fund these institutions becomes sharper. Caution should be exercised by community college administrators, however, in the interpretation and use of cost information. For example, while there are no generally accepted measures of quality, determinants that might affect program quality include faculty effectiveness and physical facilities. It would be inappropriate, therefore, for users to assume that cost information measures quality. Professional judgment based on previous experience of student demands and other factors influencing program decisions may be a more suitable alternative to cost analysis.

As long as community college administrators and managers are cognizant of the proper use of cost information and analyses, the value of such information to the decision-making process in all areas throughout the institutional system will be greatly enhanced. Accurate accounting information provides an effective management tool, but it cannot act as a substitute for good management.

References

Ameiss, A. P., and Kargas, N. A. *Accountant's Desk Handbook.* Englewood Cliffs, N.J.: Prentice-Hall, 1981

Ebey, C. "Why Don't Colleges Depreciate Fixed Assets?" *Management Accounting,* 1982, *64* (2), 13–17.

Horngren, C. T. *Cost Accounting: A Managerial Emphasis.* Englewood Cliffs, N.J.: Prentice-Hall, 1972.

Hyatt, J. A. *A Cost-Accounting Handbook for Colleges and Universities.* Washington, D.C.: National Association of College and University Business Officers, 1983.

Milesell, R. M., and Hay, L. E. *Governmental Accounting.* 3rd ed. Homewood, Illinois: Richard D. Irwin, Inc., 1961.

National Association of College and University Business Officers. *Costing for Policy Analysis.* Washington, D.C.: National Association of College and University Business Officers, 1980.

Scheps, C., and Davidson, E. E. *Accounting for Colleges and Universities.* Baton Rouge: Louisiana State University Press, 1978.

Ann L. Kaneklides is a certified public accountant and is a staff associate in the Department of Adult and Community College Education, North Carolina State University, Raleigh.

Cost-effective programs can be developed during difficult economic times if the basic elements of purchasing and maintenance programs can be agreed upon by the college.

Reaffirming Some Basic Principles in Purchasing and Maintenance

Harold L. Throop, Jr.

It is in vogue in today's college administrative aisles to suggest new and innovative ways to solve a college's purchasing and maintenance problems. From a practical point of view, the discussion within any college administrative staff should focus on the basic elements necessary for the successful operation of these programs. Without a proper base, new and innovative concepts added to these systems may merely compound existing problems. Therefore, this chapter first provides a reaffirmation of some of the basic elements that have proved necessary for the successful operation of purchasing and maintenance programs.

Then we discuss some of the concepts in purchasing and maintenance that are enabling some colleges to save much-needed operating funds. The concepts covered here are only examples of the many possible ones because the needs and the legal requirements of each college differ widely from state to state, and a complete list, for all practical purposes, would be endless.

D. Campbell (Ed.). *Strengthening Financial Management.* New Directions for
Community Colleges, no. 50. San Francisco: Jossey-Bass, June 1985.

Purchasing

Many colleges profess to have installed a purchasing system when, in fact, they have merely an "order-placing" system in operation. Purchasing, like many functions in a college, is often the result of growth and personalities active in a given area, rather than a thoroughly planned part of the business functions of the institution. In order for a college to be cost-effective in its purchasing activities, it must institute a carefully developed plan.

Philosophy. The purchasing philosophy of a college can provide positive direction to an institution during troubled economic times. Such a statement can delineate in general terms how materials and services will be acquired for the institution. Purchasing procedures can then be developed for the implementation of the purchasing philosophy.

Many individuals in the general public believe that educational systems, including colleges, are wasteful. A definitive purchasing philosophy can be used in the defense of a college, particularly when it is requesting additional funds.

A simple statement of purchasing philosophy might read: "The Purchasing Division shall have as its basic purpose to purchase materials or services in the proper quantity and quality, to have them available at the time they are needed, and to secure them at the lowest possible price from a responsible source."

To implement the statement of philosophy, administrators might adopt a procedural statement similar to the following:

The purchase of all equipment, supplies, and services for use within the college shall be the responsibility of the Business Services Department. The authority to make such purchases shall be vested in the director of purchasing, and no other employee may obligate the district for any expenditure of funds without the prior approval of the director of purchasing or the vice-president of business services. The college may, at its discretion, decide that any obligation contracted without prior approval of the director of purchasing or the vice-president of business services will be a personal expense of the employee.

Such a statement defines everyone's role in the purchasing function within the college. This statement can also help make vendors aware that they must deal with the purchasing office and that, if they do not, the institution will not be liable for the debt incurred by the staff member.

How does this save an institution money? It establishes

parameters within which individuals must function, and it enables the institution to exercise control over the dollars expended for material and services. A good purchasing system complements the college's equipment inventory system. This is important for cost-effective utilization of the college's equipment resources and also provides a basis for insurance programs and the development of equipment replacement programs. The net result is to provide assistance in budget control. Resources can be distributed more equitably and cost centers (divisions or departments) can be held accountable for their actions.

Purchasing Calendar. As a tool to augment the purchasing philosophy and procedures of an institution, a purchasing calendar can be used to ensure the purchasing of materials and services on a timely basis while also obtaining better prices by the combining of like items. The purchasing calendar can be used as a communication tool, letting the staff know when items will be purchased and helping to ensure that items will be available in time to meet the needs of the instructional programs.

The format of the calendar is simple; it can be merely a listing by month of the date when certain commodities or services will be handled by the purchasing office. Input from the total management staff as to the appropriateness of the dates used is key to the success of the program. A purchasing calendar can also assist in preventing the "dumping" of budgets at the end of the fiscal year, since this is not a good use of financial resources!

Bidding Procedures. Many states mandate that bidding for goods and services shall take place for governmental agencies with certain specified dollar limitations. Where community colleges are a part of a total system, the bidding may be done on a statewide basis or purchasing may be performed by a centralized agency.

Bidding differs from obtaining price quotations in that bidding is a formalized process requiring advertising and announcement of the proposed action to the community. The process is designed to eliminate the placement of business based upon favoritism and pressure from special-interest groups. The college should develop a written bidding procedure that ideally is approved by the governing board so that it has the effect of law. The procedure must spell out when formalized bidding will take place, the dollar amount when bidding is required, the minimum number of days for public advertising, how the bid will be advertised, and when and how a bid will be awarded. Again, this is a communication tool that lets everyone know how the college will acquire goods and services.

The cost advantage to the college is that it encourages all interested vendors to compete, thereby helping to ensure that the college is getting the best price for the goods or services desired. It also provides the internal controls needed to prevent charges of vendor preference.

Obtaining price "quotes" or quotations is a less formalized process and can either be oral or written. Oral quotes are usually permitted for smaller expenditures with written quotations required for higher dollar amounts. The quotation system provides for greater expediency in the purchasing process while also providing documentation that various vendors and their prices were checked. Both the bidding process and the use of quotations can lend credibility to purchasing functions.

Vendor Selection. The quotation and bidding processes, coupled with local and/or state laws, pretty well dictate how vendors will be selected. But there are purchases that do not fall within these areas for which vendors must be selected. One method, which helps develop an image of impartiality in selecting vendors, is to use a vendor file. The file, maintained on a current basis, lists the performance of the various vendors. Such performance data as timeliness of delivery, quality of product delivered, response time for correcting deficiencies, responsiveness to request for prices, and ability to provide product information are among the data the purchasing office might find pertinent. Basically, the file contains objective information that can be used to select or evaluate potential vendors. One of the basic functions of a purchasing office in the maintenance of a viable purchasing activity is to keep it removed from the political arena. A system of this type helps the office achieve that goal.

Lease or Purchase. In light of today's short money supply, many institutions are exploring the possibility of leasing equipment or even facilities instead of purchasing. This is particularly true in the acquisition of data processing mainframes and large capital outlay items such as transit-type buses. The advantages to leasing or third-party leasing are several. First, leasing allows for the acquisition of property with less cash, thus making acquisition possible in cases where, if the total cash amount were required at the time of purchase, the purchase probably would not take place. Second, the prorating of the cost over a number of years provides a more realistic financial picture than one in which the acquisition cost is absorbed all in one year. Third, because technology is changing so rapidly today, particularly in data processing, leasing provides greater flexibility in making changes in equipment or facilities as needs or desires may change.

The critics charge that leasing costs more and also results in a lower equity value of the product for the college. The administration must weigh the add-on cost against the possibility of not acquiring the equipment or facility in order to determine if leasing is worth it.

Contracting Services. Along with leasing of equipment or facilities, the contracting of services can be a controversial subject for the college administration, particularly in regard to employee organizations. However, there are distinct cost savings that can accrue to the institution through contracting. Some of the services that may be included in contracting are laundry, street sweeping, trash collection, typewriter repair, and library book processing. The cost savings develop because the contract price ensures a constant unit price, while, if the function is performed by college staff, the unit price will vary depending on the volume produced by the assigned staff. Another cost savings occurs in equipment replacement when the contractor is required to provide the equipment.

Contracting also provides greater flexibility; it is easier to make changes with a contract service than with college personnel. And contract services can provide backup service that might not be available otherwise. Contract service permits a college to control costs in a given area, and it provides greater ease in making budget projections. From the purchasing point of view, all contract services should be put out to bid.

The critics of contract services argue that it takes work away from college staff. In some states, in fact some forms of contract services (such as custodial services) are not permitted. Some critics argue that it is more costly, but a cost analysis in most cases can disprove this claim. There is a distinct disadvantage to trying to use contract services in small or rural communities because the services may not be available or may be available only on a limited scale. In short, the institution should perform a thorough cost study to determine the feasibility of one method over the other before making any decisions about contracting.

Maintenance

The maintenance budget of most colleges is susceptible to budget reduction during difficult economic times. It is therefore probably the victim of budget reduction more than any other segment of the college operation. This is due both to the commonly held conception that certain items of maintenance can be put off until a future date and to the fact that many institutions do not have a clearly defined plan relating to maintenance. Maintenance, as distinguished from operations, relates to the repair and replacement of buildings and equipment. It may also include the care of the campus grounds. Operations pertains to the regular housekeeping functions of the institution.

Philosophy. For the successful operation of a maintenance function, the governing body of the institution needs to develop a definitive policy statement. This statement will assist the college administration in developing long-and short-range goals for the effective operation of the maintenance department and, thus, in the long run, it will help provide cost savings to the college. Basically, a policy statement assists the college in moving the management of maintenance from the crisis level to a cost-containment position. It also enables everyone connected with the institution to understand the relationship of maintenance to the total budgetary program. If a maintenance program is always reacting to a crisis situation, the result is a very costly but less than efficient maintenance program.

A statement of philosophy or policy for an institution might include the following: "The maintenance program shall give primary consideration to the preventive maintenance of the college's facilities and equipment. Every effort shall be made to ensure timely repairs of college property, and the maintenance program shall endeavor to maintain a quality level commensurate with the college's instructional program."

In order to further the implementation of the philosophy or policy of the governing board relating to maintenance, the college administration should review the value of proper maintenance to the teaching environment. Quite often in the arena of employer-employee negotiations this particular point is overlooked. A lack of response to maintenance problems can have a direct effect on employer-employee relationships. Normally, it is not a large maintenance problem that is the culprit but rather the small ones that are found in the classroom. By solving some of these minor problems, the administration can ease some of the tension present at the negotiating table. One solution to this type of irritant is to have the maintenance department send a questionnaire to each faculty member in the spring of each year. On the questionnaire, the faculty members should list any problem that they have with their teaching station, no matter how small. The maintenance department should then categorize the returns into maintenance job craft categories. These could then be analyzed as to cost and feasibility and the appropriate ones turned over to the corresponding craft to be taken care of.

Such a system can result in a higher rating for maintenance

among faculty, the elimination in an organized manner of minor maintenance problems, and a reduction in maintenance cost because of the systematic manner in which minor maintenance problems are resolved.

Budgeting for Maintenance. Budgetary planning makes possible the setting of priorities and control of resources. The following subsections offer examples of short-range and long-range planning.

Budget Guidelines. A short-range approach to maintenance planning includes the use of budget guidelines. Except in the case of emergencies such as broken pipes or gas leaks, maintenance requests (such as those for new carpeting, remodeling of offices, changing doors, and so on) consist essentially of items that the staff would like for the improvement of the environment. Budget guidelines within the overall college budget should allocate a certain amount of money annually to each department or division for this type of change. The formula for the amount allocated could be based on student full-time equivalents, number of staff, or some other common type of criteria. A review of historical expenditures in the various categories is essential to the development of the criteria. During the budgeting process, the formula, not the particular maintenance project, becomes the issue open to debate; this, in turn, provides for more responsible management since the administration of each department will be required to stay within the allocated funds. The guidelines also act as a communication tool, making everyone aware of limited resources and overall college goals. For example, a budget guideline can be implemented to protect the quality of the campus grounds and to provide a tool for the evaluation of management personnel.

Five-Year Plan. The long-range plan can utilize a five-year projection (or any other number of years desired) in order to facilitate the scheduling of more expensive maintenance items. For instance, to try to replace all roofs or resurface all blacktop in one year is cost prohibitive, but to develop a schedule that allocates a given amount of fiscal resources each year to a specified project is feasible in most cases. The plan allows for the projection of costs and the prioritizing of proposed expenditures, and it places the maintenance budget within the arena of overall budget development for the colleges.

Work-Force Analysis. Quite often in the development of a maintenance department, new positions are created for a specific task but then these positions are not reviewed in light of ongoing need. A work-force analysis should be conducted to determine the

appropriateness of the staff organization. In the analysis, consideration should be given to actual hours available to perform work by the
total work force. A monthly review of the total hours available less
breaks, vacations, and sick leave will provide information as to
whether the maintenance department can actually accomplish
assigned tasks on a timely basis. If the total net hours available are not
sufficient to perform the assigned tasks, the department then has such
options as adding appropriate staff, reducing the number of projects,
or considering outside contracting for the desired projects. A work-
force analysis also provides for a realistic approach to preparing
timelines for the completion of designated projects.

Trends for Stabilizing Costs. One of the most talked about costs
relating to the operation of colleges is that of utilities. Whether the
utilities bills consist of electricity, fuel oil, gas, or telephones, there
seems to be a guaranteed annual increase in these items. Many institutions are attempting to contain costs through various methods; the
following paragraphs briefly describe some of these methods.

Solar Energy. Solar energy is a very popular "new" energy
source, particularly in the Sun Belt and the West. Installation can be
either expensive or inexpensive based upon the number and expertise of the college personnel involved. Solar energy is well suited to
providing a heat source for swimming pools, showers, and the hot-
water needs of a cafeteria. The cost variables involve the support
structure, solar panels, storage tanks, and the pumps. If existing
storage tanks and piping can be utilized, the cost of installation will
decrease appreciably. Solar panels differ in design and cost; institution's needs should be analyzed carefully before the panels are
selected.

The creation of a solar system provides an excellent learning
experience for students involved in related classes and for skilled
maintenance personnel to work together in creating a viable new
source of energy at an affordable cost. (Some colleges that have
developed a system in this way are willing to give advice to interested
institutions.) In addition, the coordinated effort of students and staff
provides an excellent opportunity for positive public relations with
the general public.

Energy Management. Energy management can take a number of
forms; the one most often discussed utilizes a microcomputer system
to regulate the flow of electrical energy on campus. The system can
turn on or off lights, fans, motors, and air-conditioning and heating
units as well as many other items. Such a system can be either very
simple or very complex depending on the availability of funds and the

desires of the institution. Normally, fans, motors, and compressors are the first items managed by such a system. As additional needs arise or funds become available, new items can be placed under the system's control. It is ideal for shutting down equipment when there is no need for its operation (for example, on weekends).

The installation of the system, like the solar energy system, can be accomplished by staff and could involve the appropriate participation from industry and technology students. The payback to the institution in the control of energy is very high. The major caution is for the institution to be sure to select a basic system for which parts will be available in four or five years; some of the products currently on the market gradually become obsolete.

Telephone System. With the breakup of the telephone monopoly, many colleges have acquired their own telephone system. The main advantage lies in the stabilization of costs. The main disadvantage is the cash outlay needed to purchase a system if the institution does not enter into a lease-with-option-to-purchase contract. Available for most telephone systems is a call-accounting system that permits the recording of all calls made from the user's extension. An analysis can be made of who is making long-distance calls and these calls can then be charged to the user's extension when appropriate. The system also permits budgeting by cost centers for the cost of the telephone use.

A disadvantage that must be considered in acquiring a telephone system is the maintenance of the system. Will a college use its own staff, or will it contract for the service? Contract service is expensive, but the quality of maintenance by college staff could be questionable.

Deferred Maintenance. "Deferred maintenance" can have several meanings. It can indicate that a maintenance item will be deferred to some time in the future because it has been incorporated into a long-range plan. Another meaning, and the one most prevalent today, is that a maintenance project will be deferred until some time in the future because of the current lack of funds. Unfortunately, the maintenance budget is often used as part of the balancing act when funds must be cut from the college budget. This is not always wise or appropriate. It may enable the college to balance its budget, but it may also seriously impair the effective use of a facility or a piece of equipment. It is also most likely to cost a great deal more when the item is repaired or replaced at some time in the future. Furthermore, some repair work that is deferred may cost more to repair in the future not just because of inflation but because more deterioration may have occurred. The deferring of maintenance expenditures as well as some

42

other types of expenditures has caused a number of states to mandate differential funding for postsecondary institutions. This ensures that some dollars will flow to the maintenance of facilities that are worth millions to taxpayers.

In deferring maintenance in order to balance a budget or to provide salary increases, the administration often overlooks the effect of poor maintenance on the education environment. The quality of teaching suffers if maintenance is not performed in a timely manner. In order to provide a professional approach to this subject, administrators must develop both a short-range and a long-range program for maintenance. Such programs can allow the deferring of maintenance based on priorities. A maintenance program that operates only on a fiscal-year basis will be devastated when and if deferred maintenance is put into place.

Summary

New possibilities in purchasing and maintenance are achievable if the institution first develops a base upon which it can build these programs. Ideas change and new technology is constantly being developed, but these items will not be of lasting use to a college in difficult economic times unless the college has developed and agreed upon the basic elements of a purchasing program and a maintenance program.

Harold L. Throop, Jr. is vice-president of business for El Camino Community College District in Torrance, California.

As federal sources of student aid decrease and costs increase, higher education seeks new sources of financial aid funding.

Developing New Sources of Student Financial Aid

David R. Bauske

Student financial aid plays a significant role in the success of community colleges today. If their mission of providing access to higher education to all segments of their communities is to be realized, the colleges must do more than merely open their doors. They must assist financially needy students in meeting the costs that accompany access to higher education. An open-door admissions policy truly provides access to higher education only when supported by a strong student financial assistance program.

The office of student financial aid is one of the newer administrative branches at most community colleges. Federal student financial aid did not exist in any form until the GI bill following World War II. It was not until 1958 that Congress approved the first major federal student assistance program. This was the Sputnik-inspired National Defense Education Act, which funded low-interest student loans primarily to engineering, math, and science students. It was not until the passage of the Basic Educational Opportunity Grant (BEOG) program in 1972 that the majority of community college campuses created financial aid offices. In the dozen years since the implementation of the BEOG program (renamed Pell Grants in 1980), the

D. Campbell (Ed.). *Strengthening Financial Management.* New Directions for Community Colleges, no. 50. San Francisco: Jossey-Bass, June 1985.

importance of the financial aid office to the success of the college has increased dramatically.

Financial Aid Funding

Administering student financial aid is "big business." Estimates of the total amount of student financial aid available for the 1984–85 academic year range as high as $18 billion (College Entrance Examination Board, 1984, p. 2). Of this figure, 51.7 percent is disbursed to students in the form of loans, 44.6 percent is grants, and 3.7 percent is work aid (p. 4). Ten years earlier (1975–76), approximately $10.5 billion were available (Gillespie and Carlson, 1983, p. 5).

These total dollar figures mask what has actually happened to the level of funding for financial aid during the past decade. When the figures for total funding are converted into constant 1982 dollars, the years of greater funding are reversed. Funding for the academic year 1975–76 in constant dollars equates to 18.1 billion (Gillespie and Carlson, 1983, p. 6) while funding for the academic year 1984–85 drops to $16.3 billion (College Entrance Examination Board, 1984, p. 6). This represents a dramatic decrease in the amount of money available per student when one considers the increased costs of attendance at institutions and the significantly larger national student body.

Costs and Awards. Financial aid is generally awarded to cover both the direct costs of attending college (tuition, fees, books, supplies) and the indirect costs (room, board, personal expenses, transportation). The average nine-month cost of attendance at this nation's community colleges has risen from $1,386 in 1975–76 (Gillespie and Carlson, 1983, p. 20) to $2,560 in 1983–84 (College Entrance Examination Board, 1984, p. 9). This represents approximately an 85 percent increase in the average cost of attendance. During this same period, however, the average amount of financial aid awarded at all types of institutions per one full-time equivalent student (FTE) rose from $1,236 in 1975–76 to $1,950 in 1983–84 (Gillespie and Carlson, 1983, p. 20; College Entrance Examination Board, 1984, p. 9). Therefore, the amount of financial aid awarded per FTE rose slightly less than 58 percent during a period when college costs escalated by 85 percent. If the amount of the average financial aid award per FTE were viewed in constant dollars, the figure would drop from $2,151 in 1975–76 to $1,851 in 1983–84. Clearly the large total amount of financial aid available today does not indicate that students are receiving awards sufficient to cover their college costs.

Community College Aid Share. Because of the low-cost nature of community colleges, they generally do not accumulate the institutional financial aid funds that are found at many four-year public institutions and most private colleges and universities. Only recently have many community colleges initiated institutional development projects and alumni contacts. These two areas, which have generated millions of dollars for the financial aid programs of private colleges and universities, have been virtually ignored by the community colleges. It is the institutional financial aid funds, such as scholarships funded by development projects and alumni, that provide financial aid offices with the flexibility necessary to serve students with unusual talents, circumstances, or abilities.

It is not just in the area of institutionally generated financial aid funding that the community colleges appear to receive less funding than other institutions. A study conducted by Nelson (1980) found that community college students appear to receive less than their fair share of federal campus-based aid (such as College Work Study, National Direct Student Loans, and Supplemental Educational Opportunity Grants) and of state aid in comparison with their counterparts at other institutions. This inequity does not appear to be present in the receipt of Pell Grants. No cause could be pinpointed for the community colleges' diminished share of campus-based and state financial aid funds. However, one possible reason is the expertise of the community college financial aid officer. Nelson found that, for all types of institutions at any enrollment level, "the aid officer at the community college does tend to be the least experienced and to have the smallest staff" (p. 40).

Impact of Current Funding. The current level of federal and state financial aid funding indicates that students are not as well off comparatively as in previous years. As college costs continue to rise, federal funding has continued at more or less a steady level. Therefore, each year that same financial aid funding loses ground to increasing costs, and more and more students are forced to make unpleasant educational decisions.

If community colleges cannot find the funds to meet a student's needs, several alternatives exist for the student. He or she can reduce the number of credit hours attempted and work for additional money. The student may stop out entirely for a length of time to work and then return for a period. This cycle can then be repeated. The student can "shop around" for a different institution with a more adequate supply of financial aid funds. Or the student may simply give up on the idea of going to college at that time. If this happens, the likelihood of the student ever returning to college is reduced. The optimum time to be able to meet a student's needs is when he or she is eager to enter an institution. A severe disappointment, such as an insufficient financial aid package, greatly reduces the chances that the student will try again. Thus, adequate financial aid can be as important to many students as the community college open door.

Developing Sources of Funds

The total amount of funding for student aid from all sources (federal, state, institutional, and private) is declining. The one source that is demonstrating considerable growth is the private sector, represented primarily by foundations and businesses that support education (Hall, 1984). Because of their local nature, community colleges have the ability and the background to work with regional foundations, businesses, and industries to secure additional financial aid funding for their students. Also, at the local level, community colleges have the ability (whether exercised or not) to undertake development activities designed to increase their institutional student aid funds. At the state and, particularly, the federal level, individual colleges exercise little influence over student aid funding; however, when their voices are joined in organizations such as the American Association of Community and Junior Colleges (AACJC), they can better influence the legislative process. Despite strong efforts by the AACJC, the National Association of Student Financial Aid Administrators (NASFAA), the American Council on Education (ACE), and many other similar organizations, the total student aid funding level is inadequate and the future looks no brighter. Gladieux (1983) emphasizes this view in discussing the future of student financial aid: "One thing is clear. There will not be enough money to go all the way around in the coming years" (p. 422).

Local Initiatives. There appear to be two approaches that colleges are taking in order to maximize their financial aid funding and help students remain in school even if the amount of student aid available is not adequate. These approaches are (1) developing new local sources of financial aid funding and (2) developing flexible payment plans that allow students some additional options for meeting their college cost obligations.

Most community colleges are likely to be able to develop initiatives that can result in increasing their institutional financial aid funding and in increasing their students' share of private financial aid funds. Because of the community-oriented focus and flexibility of these institutions, they have the ability to develop and promote projects that can demonstrate their value to significant community segments. Projects to develop new sources of student aid funds usually rely on strong institutional leadership and support from the entire college. Rarely can the administration of a financial aid office generate the staff time and institutional support necessary to "sell" community funding of student financial aid without active college executive leadership. Certainly this is as it should be because student financial aid administration affects almost every segment of the institution, including admissions, student retention, budgeting, public relations, development, student services, and financial management.

Colleges develop funding sources by promoting the successful programs they have. Success stories tend to generate more success stories. For example, if a local corporation has hired several community college graduates from the electronics program and they have proved to be productive employees, the corporation may be convinced by college personnel to sponsor a scholarship for electronics students. By supporting the electronics program through student financial aid, the corporation may be helping to ensure itself a quality employee pool. Similarly, if the corporation enjoys success with the scholarship arrangement, it could be approached to support aid funding for other programs from which it may hire employees— such as secretarial science, advertising, or middle management. Ultimately, if the relationship between the corporation and the college remains strong, the college could approach the corporation for unrestricted student aid funding. By this time, the corporation has had evidence that the college develops well-educated students through a number of programs and should be willing to establish an ongoing partnership of support.

Funding Sources. Community colleges have a number of potential funding sources available to them. Included among these are businesses and industries, community organizations, foundations, unions, interested citizens, alumni, and even themselves. Although individuals within the college may approach whatever potential source of funds they think best, all approaches should be endorsed by the institutional leadership and coordinated to prevent duplication and the appearance of disorganization.

Business and Industry. As mentioned in the previous subsection, business and industry have the potential to provide funding for both restricted and unrestricted scholarships. Businesses and industries are not charitable organizations. They will want to see the potential for benefits to themselves from their contributions. Certainly the college can provide well-educated employees for these organizations; in addition the college can sometimes establish specific courses required by the organization for its current employees. Often, the fact that the local community contains a quality educational institution makes it easier for businesses and industries to recruit and retain quality employees. Thus, any collegiate approach to business should be predicated on the fact that the college can provide a substantial return for a business investment in student financial aid.

An example of a community college that has successfully developed a scholarship program utilizing funds from business and industry is Tompkins-Cortland Community College. The college utilizes tax-deductible contributions from various industries to award scholarships for industry employees who want to further their educations (College of New Rochelle and The College Board, 1983).

Community Organizations. Every community has a number of service and charitable organizations that provide scholarships or other forms of student assistance to local students. This source of student aid funding is probably the most difficult to cultivate because it is the least systematized (Huff, 1983). Among the many potential scholarship donors are Rotary clubs, Elks, Jaycees, chambers of commerce, Knights of Columbus, 4-H clubs, the PTA, and many other fraternities and sororities. Community colleges can gain access to most of these aid sources by actively publicizing the existence and scope of the college's financial aid program. Financial aid administrators should personalize relations with these organizations by seeking public-speaking opportunities and providing financial aid success stories.

Foundations. Charitable foundations continue to provide millions of dollars in student financial aid each year. However, with the decreases in federal and state aid funding, the competition for foundation money is extremely fierce. Local foundations may provide the greatest opportunity for a community college to secure additional financial aid funds for the same reason local industries contribute— the local community is aware of the institution's successes and its ongoing commitment to enhancing life within the community. Any attempts to secure funds from a national foundation must be undertaken as a college commitment, not just as a financial aid office quest. Foundations and their various activities can be identified in several ways. The Foundation Center (1984) publishes the *Foundation Directory* that lists all large foundations in the country and their primary funding activities. Colleges can also discover what institutions have received grants from various foundations by reading the *Chronicle of Higher Education*.

Unions. Often labor unions offer scholarships either to their members or to the sons and daughters of members. Similarly, many unions have bargained for tuition benefits from their employers. Surprisingly, "employees rarely use the amount of money earmarked in corporate budgets" (Gladieux, 1983, p. 415). One way, therefore, that community colleges can benefit from this unused source of aid is to promote their educational opportunities to union members who have tuition benefits as part of their contracts.

Colleges can also explore other ways to make the return to college more attractive for employed workers. For example, the College of New Rochelle defers tuition payments for students who present documentation that they will receive employee reimbursement (College of New Rochelle and The College Board, 1983). In this way, the student does not need to commit his or her own funds while waiting for the reimbursement to arrive.

Interested Citizens and Alumni. It is only recently that most community colleges have become actively involved in development and alumni activities. These activities have provided millions of dollars to private colleges over the years, and it is surprising that only now are most community colleges becoming involved. Development and alumni work can be utilized to identify potential donors to the college's student aid funds. Although identifying donors is usually the result of the work of a number of individuals, it is often best for one college representative to explain the benefits of student financial aid to the donor. Particularly in the case of interested citizens who did not go through the college, it is essential that they thoroughly understand the good that aid does and the students it can support. After a contribution has been made, the financial aid office should keep the donor apprised as to the awarding of the funds and the benefits the student or students are enjoying as a result.

Alumni tracking can lead to additional student aid funding. Successful alumni who valued their experience at college are more easily persuaded to contribute to an aid fund than strangers to the process. Also, scholarships can be established and funded by each graduating class. A group contribution can yield significant benefits when individual contributions would not be enough for a continuing scholarship.

Colleges. Colleges themselves contribute a great deal to financial aid programs both in terms of money and administrative efforts to keep needy students enrolled. Generally, community colleges have fewer institutional funds available for student aid than other types of institutions. However, the use of these funds is limited only by ingenuity.

Many colleges have developed additional financial aid sources from within themselves. For example, the Community College of Philadelphia has created an emergency loan fund by accumulating the college application fees. Another example of creative use of institutional funds is Beloit College's "world obligation scholarships." These are basically loans that carry only a moral obligation to repay. They are repaid through tax-deductible contributions to the fund. The fund is expected to expand constantly since many former students continue to contribute beyond the end of their obligation (College of New Rochelle and The College Board, 1983). Institutional funds are rarely subject to the regulations that restrict federal aid funds, and this freedom can stimulate the administration's imagination in finding creative uses for these funds.

Alternatives to Expanded Aid

Most community colleges do not have enough institutional student aid funds to create many meaningful options for their students. However, they do have some flexibility in collecting student payments. Among the various payment plans found at colleges across the country are discounts on tuition for such reasons as the enrollment of multiple family members, the prepayment of a full year's tuition, or the recruitment of other students. Also, paying tuition and fees on the installment plan is becoming more common. In most cases, this allows students to make payments at regular intervals throughout the semester. Many colleges allow credit card payments. In fact, DeVry Institute issues its own credit card, which allows students to pay their tuition on credit and repay the debt at a percentage rate considerably below regular bank credit card rates.

An alternative form of financial aid can be found in granting credit by examination. Academically superior students can "test out" of many hours of college work, thereby saving themselves the cost of attendance for those hours. Community colleges should be certain that their credit-by-examination policies are clear and realistic. Community colleges can also encourage students to consider flexible work study approaches whereby they alternate terms of work with terms of study. Community colleges already do a better job of dealing with alternate periods of work and study than do other types of institutions. Finally, community colleges should develop brochures and presentations to help interested students live frugally while they are enrolled. Consumer education should be part of a college education, and, if some tips on smart shopping, purchases to be postponed, or getting the most apartment for your dollar, can help a few students remain in college, then the distribution of this information will be worth the effort.

Summary

Community college students are being squeezed in the vise of decreasing student financial aid funds and increasing college costs. While there is little that individual colleges can do to increase federal and state funding, there are areas they can pursue to develop new sources of student financial aid. With a united institutional leadership, colleges can seek funds successfully from businesses and industries, community organizations, foundations, unions, and interested citizens and alumni. In seeking donations from the latter two sources, the community college would be well served by an active development and alumni program. Community colleges can also look within themselves to find ways of utilizing the funds that they have for student needs. They can also explore alternative student payment strategies and institutional initiatives to help students remain enrolled despite decreasing financial aid awards.

Community colleges hold out the hope of a college education for millions of students. It is up to the leaders of those institutions to develop the resources necessary to keep that hope alive.

References

College Entrance Examination Board. *Trends in Student Aid: 1980 to 1984.* New York: College Entrance Examination Board, 1984.

College of New Rochelle and The College Board. *Improving Financial Aid Services for Adults: A Program Guide.* New York: College Entrance Examination Board, 1983.

Gillespie, D. A., and Carlson, N. *Trends in Student Aid: 1963 to 1983.* New York: College Entrance Examination Board, 1983.

Gladieux, L. E. "Future Directions of Student Aid." In R. H. Fenske, R. P. Huff, and Associates (Eds.), *Handbook of Student Financial Aid: Programs, Procedures, and Policies.* San Francisco: Jossey-Bass, 1983.

Hall, D. "New Rules and New Players in the Game." *Change,* 1984, *16* (8), 35–37.

Huff, R. "Expanding and Utilizing Private and Institutional Sources of Aid." In R. H. Fenske, R. P. Huff, and Associates (Eds.), *Handbook of Student Financial Aid: Programs, Procedures, and Policies.* San Francisco: Jossey-Bass, 1983.

52

Nelson, S. C. *Community Colleges and Their Share of Student Financial Assistance.* New York: College Entrance Examination Board, 1980.

The Foundation Center. *The Foundation Directory.* 9th ed. New York: Columbia University Press, 1984.

David R. Bauske is the director for financial aid services in The College Board's southwestern regional office, Austin, Texas.

Part 2.
The Shift to an Entrepreneurial Team

The key to efficient and effective use of limited resources is environmental scanning coupled with sound program planning.

Institutional Research: A Critical Component of Sound Financial Planning

John T. Blong
Adelbert J. Purga

The 1980s will be known either as the era of retrenchment and exigency or as the era of planning in higher education. It will all depend on how higher education reacts to the multitude of problems now facing our institutions.

To understand the problems, we need to view the past as it relates to the reality of the present. In the plush times of the sixties, we dealt with problems of growth. The economy was expanding, enrollment of eighteen- to twenty-four-year-olds grew from 18 to 34 percent of the population, and both government and private donors were investing in higher education. It was truly the Golden Era. A new community college opened every two weeks, and major construction was taking place on almost every campus. We thought that good times would never end, and all of our planning (if it deserved to be called such) involved which land to buy, where to excavate, or which degree program to institute (Strohm, 1983).

D. Campbell (Ed.). *Strengthening Financial Management.* New Directions for Community Colleges, no. 50. San Francisco: Jossey-Bass, June 1985.

Then came the decline of the Golden Era in the mid seventies. It was the end of the period of expansion and the beginning of the era of retrenchment, although at that time no one really understood the enormous implications of the turnabout in statistics (Devoky, 1979). The baby boomers were gone, the economy had slowed, inflation was rampant, and the esteem of higher education was at a low ebb.

At first, the education establishment ignored the problems, but effects of the decline began to have impact almost immediately. Poor fiscal management during the sixties had left the education community in no better shape than it was prior to that time. Bowen (1970) best described fiscal planning of the Golden Era when he said, "The basic principle of college finance is very simple. Institutions raise as much money as they can get and spend it all" (p. 81).

This lack of financial planning in times of plenty led to an emphasis on financial planning in the late seventies and early eighties. The need was critical for solid management and planning, but, because of higher education's laissez-faire policies of the past, none of the skills had been developed. As Keller (1983) suggested, "the era of laissez-faire campus administration is over. The era of academic strategy has begun" (p. 26).

Higher education first looked to business and industry for solutions. Seeing the problem as one of dwindling resources, education reached for the solutions of efficiency that the private sector had to offer. Strategies such as the Planning-Programming-Budgeting System (PPBS) and zero-base budgeting (ZBB) were being instituted throughout the country at an unprecedented pace. The educational administrators of the seventies were going to control their way out of the economic plight within their institution. With these new tools from industry, they were convinced they could cut expenses and make their current programs efficient enough to weather the financial storm.

This new approach to managing decline was only marginally successful. It did move many institutions from organized anarchies with "tooth fairy" mentalities to institutions with internal accountability. The educational community was looking at itself from the point of view of efficiency; specifically, it was asking itself, "In what manner and quantity are we utilizing our resources?"

This advancement in educational management (the use of internal program evaluation that includes tactical planning, fiscal decision making, and accountability) may only have moved institutions from exigency to a state of stringency—and a degradation of quality. The focus was on efficiency measures, not effectiveness measures.

The reliance on efficiency measures has caused institutions to focus on short-term goals, such as decreasing unit cost and increasing student-teacher ratios. This short-term approach to program planning may in fact be in conflict with the true goals of education, which are normally long-term change in both students and society. The missing element in the approach to program evaluation is a commitment to a focus on the effectiveness of the offerings, which leads us to evaluate the long-term outcomes and values of our program offerings to both the student and the community.

In other words, the missing elements in renewing the health of higher education are an awareness of the external environment as well as the internal environment and a commitment to react to both. This ability to react can only be accomplished by establishing program evaluation systems that deal with both efficiency and effectiveness.

Program Evaluation

Program evaluation has taken on a heightened significance in institutional planning. Craven (1980) defines program evaluation as "the process of specifying, defining, collecting, analyzing, and interpreting information about designated aspects of a given program and using that information to arrive at value judgments among decision alternatives regarding the installation, continuation, modification, or termination of a program" (p. 434). Consistent with Craven's definition, the function of institutional research becomes paramount as we require information about our programs, both current and future.

The actual process of program evaluation thus embodies two major areas of analyses: efficiency and effectiveness. Various financially based models are available to aid decision makers in determining a program's efficiency. As significant as the traditionally based efficiency measures, however, is the provision of data that allow informed decisions on curriculum effectiveness. As offered in the monograph "Postsecondary Program Evaluation," published by the National Postsecondary Alliance (1981), many models exist that can be modified to apply to local needs. Examples of these models can be found at Brevard Community College, Caldwell Community College, Midlands Area Technical College, School of Technical Careers at Southern Illinois University, Trident Technical College, and Utah Technical College in Provo.

As we begin to formulate a program evaluation activity, the institutional research function becomes key to the collection, analysis, and synthesis of various data elements related to external and internal factors. External factors are examined usually through a process called needs assessment or environmental scanning, which will be discussed later in this chapter. The objectives of program evaluation relate to the following areas:

1. Program development activities: These include looking at the nature of each program—length of time required for a degree, admissions requirements, components of the program courses in relation to employment standards, and relationship of the program to emerging changes in the occupational field.

2. Curricula improvements: The breadth and scope of the curricula should be examined in relation to general education and institutional degree requirements, and the potential of alternative instructional delivery techniques for improving the learning environments should be considered.

3. Physical facilities improvements: These assessments cover the current state of facilities and the projected need for addition or replacement, including such items as adequacy of space, heating, air conditioning, ventilation, safety, and lighting.

4. Equipment: The evaluation should look at both the current status of equipment and projected need, including replacement. Is the institution's equipment comparable in type and quality found in the job market?

5. Supplies and materials: What is the current state as regards quantity, relevance to industrial use, quality, and cost of materials and supplies needed for program training?

6. Learning resource center needs: The evaluation should cover such support services as the library and media services.

7. Industrial standards versus institutional program standards: Are the program exit competencies relevant to industrial entry competencies?

8. Job placement: What success have graduates had in acquiring jobs and in keeping jobs? Elements of this assessment might include graduates' longevity in job and job advancement.

9. Personnel planning: These assessments include the range of faculty and staff qualifications, potential for development, turnover rates, workload criteria, evaluation criteria, and cost.

10. Future occupational trends: The institution should look at employment trends in the marketplace, particularly as they relate to new programming or adaptation of existing programming.

11. Enrollment patterns and projections: Enrollment figures

can be broken down into categories of past, present, and future, full-time and part-time, completion rates, and special populations.

Traditionally based evaluation models have focused on such factors as physical facilities, equipment, materials and supplies, faculty, enrollment, and enrollment projections. In an environment such as we find in the 1980s and project for the 1990s, these factors must be supplemented by effectiveness measures if decision makers are to ensure the viability and success of academic programming—that is, if programs are to be beneficial to the student seeking employment or continued education. These effectiveness measures include analyses of program development, curriculum improvement, industrial standards versus institutional program standards, job placement, and future occupational trends. Obviously, when we begin to investigate effectiveness, we can no longer monitor only institutionally based data. We must begin to learn from the external environment whether that environment be defined as economic, political, cultural, social, or competitive.

The use of external as well as internal measures helps decision makers to bridge the information gap between community needs and college services and to assess both where the institution is and where it must be to serve effectively the needs of its constituency, both current and future. We can no longer rely totally on internal measures typically defined in the realm of financial flexibility. We must now identify trends in the external environment and the implications to our program decision making. There is no question as to the continued significance of the role of the financial decision maker in any program evaluation model. Our challenge for institutional research in fact is, and will continue to be, to provide financial decision makers as well as curricula decision makers with valid internal and external information related to academic programming. "As planning and budgeting are increasingly integrated, the institutional research function is likely to become more prominent and more decision oriented" (Orwig and Caruthers, 1980, p. 360).

Successful program evaluation is contingent upon useful, current information from the marketplace. These data, often provided through a needs assessment process, will aid the institutional decision makers in determining if an existing program should be continued, deleted, or modified regardless of its cost efficiency. It will also provide insight as to what emerging curriculum areas the institution may wish to activate.

Community needs assessment can be an expensive

undertaking, especially if outside consultants are contracted to implement the process. Many successful needs assessments have been fully implemented utilizing an institution's own staff and resources, thus keeping the cost to a minimum. One of the benefits of conducting one's own needs assessment is the involvement of the staff in the process rather than only in the outcomes of the activity. As we focus on the development of institutional cyclic planning processes, needs assessment will provide us with information that will allow congruence between the needed services of the college's clientele and the college's offerings and aid in the development of appropriate and timely institutional goals. By using needs assessment as a two-way communication channel between the constituency and the institution, we will find ourselves in a better position to interpret employment information and thus to align our services and offerings accurately. The needs assessment information that follows focuses on the typical techniques of data collection, typical community target groups (constituencies), the typical data collection technique used for each target group, and a set of recommended procedures for conducting a needs assessment.

Five commonly used techniques for data collection are the survey, social indicators, key informant, community forum, and rates-under-treatment approaches (Warheit, Bell, and Schwab, 1975). The two most frequently used types of data collection are the social indicators approach and the survey. The social indicators approach allows us to draw inferences of need from descriptive data, such as the United States census and federal, state, local and agency reports. The social indicators technique should be conducted prior to any other technique so that the researcher may develop needs assessment analysis goals and hypothesize potential conclusions. The survey technique involves the collection of data from a sample of an entire population. The most common methods used with the survey technique are personal interviews, telephone interviews, and mail questionnaires. If conducted with properly developed and tested methods, the survey technique can be the most scientifically valid method of evaluating programs or determining needs.

The third type of data collection technique is the key informant approach. This approach utilizes individuals who are most aware of constituency needs. As the name implies, the key informant approach most often involves personal interviews or telephone interviews. Key informants may also be used in the fourth type of data collection, the community forum. In the community forum, individuals are invited to participate in a large meeting with the goal of identifying the needs of the service area. The community forum can also increase the involvement in the institution of key community individuals.

The fifth type of data collection is rates-under-treatment. In this approach, we typically monitor the rates of various agencies and institutions within our service area to determine the health of those institutions. For example, the census patterns within the hospitals, nursing homes, and other health agencies in the community can indicate the need for a nursing or allied health program. If these institutions' occupancy rate has been decreasing and is currently at a low level, we may infer that the potential employment of our college's graduates in the health area may be minimal. Most needs assessments are conducted by utilizing a combination of these data collection methods for each target group. "Target group," or "constituency" refers to the homogeneous groupings of clientele that may benefit from institutional services. Once constituency groups are identified, representatives from that constituency group should be invited to participate in the needs assessment activity. When communication channels between various constituency groups and the institution are utilized, the market data collection will contribute to the strategic planning efforts in ensuring the meeting of the clientele needs and goals. The following represents a typical list of constituency groups for a community college (this list is not to be viewed as all inclusive): business and industry, government agencies, high schools, human services organizations, minority groups, senior citizens, service or civic organizations, and present students. The following represents suggested data collection methods for each of these target groups: business and industry—key informant; government agencies—key informant and rates-under-treatment; high schools—survey; human service organizations—key informant, rates-under-treatment, and survey; minority groups—key informant, social indicators, and surveys; senior citizens—key informant, social indicators, and survey; present students—survey; service or civic organizations—key informant, rates-under-treatment, and survey.

Successful needs assessments have been conducted by institutions utilizing their own staff and resources by adhering to the following steps:

1. A needs assessment committee should be established within the institution with the purpose of identifying constituency groups.

2. The needs assessment committee then publishes the list of

constituency groups throughout the organization for validation. If deemed necessary, this process can be repeated using the Delphi technique until general consensus is achieved.

3. Once constituency-group validation is achieved, the needs assessment committee selects representatives for a community forum. Each representative is typically a key informant with expertise pertaining to a particular constituency group.

4. When the community forum is convened, each group of constituency representatives becomes a subcommittee; the subcommittee's goal is to recommend the appropriate method for data collection and perhaps propose what accomplishments are expected.

5. The office of institutional research or some other representatives of the institution then proceed in the data collection process relating to each target group.

6. Once the data collection methods have been implemented, the office of institutional research analyzes and synthesizes the information and prepares it for discussion by a reconvened community forum.

7. The community forum provides recommendations based on the report from the institutional research office and these recommendations are then presented to the institution's key decision makers.

Once the original community needs assessment has been conducted, we have set the scene for cyclic needs assessments. Each year the listing of constituency groups should be validated, and each year the institution should assess a portion of the constituency groups. Thus, a three-year cyclic pattern for the needs assessment process can be established. Under this model we will be communicating with each constituency group once every three years, allowing us timely information so that we may make informed decisions regarding our curricula.

Summary

In this chapter, we have tried to focus on the critical nature of informed decision making, particularly as it relates to institutional vitality. Only by a clear understanding of the needs of the community can a community college allocate its resources in an appropriate and effective manner to enable the accomplishment of its mission. Since a majority of an institution's resources are allocated to curricular offerings, program evaluation becomes a vital link in determining the value of existing programs as well as the emerging needs for new programs. Needs assessment, then, has become a new dimension of the institutional research job. We must be in a position to incorporate information about the institution's clientele and the institution itself into delivery systems, operational strategies, and strategic planning. Needs assessment, or market research, is a vital communications process between the service area and the institution.

References

Bowen, H. "Financial Needs of the Campus." In R. Connery (Ed.), *The Corporation and the Campus.* New York: Academy of Political Science, 1970.

Craven, E. "Evaluating Program Performance." In P. Jedamus, M. W. Peterson, and Associates, (Eds.), *Improving Academic Management: A Handbook of Planning and Institutional Research.* San Francisco: Jossey-Bass, 1980.

Devoky, D. "Burden of the Seventies: The Management of Decline." *Phi Delta Kappan,* Oct. 1979, pp. 87–91.

Keller, G. *Academic Strategy: The Management Revolution in American Higher Education.* Baltimore, Md.: Johns Hopkins University Press, 1983.

National Postsecondary Alliance. "Postsecondary Program Evaluation." Columbus: National Center for Research in Vocational Education, Ohio State University, 1981.

Orwig, M. D., and Caruthers, J. D. "Selecting Budget Strategies and Priorities." In P. Jedamus, M. W. Peterson, and Associates (Eds.), *Improving Academic Management: A Handbook of Planning and Institutional Research.* San Francisco: Jossey-Bass, 1980.

Strohm, P. "Faculty Roles Today and Tomorrow." *Academe,* Jan.-Feb. 1983, pp. 10–15.

Warheit, G. J., Bell, R. A., and Schwab, J. J. *Planning for Change: Needs Assessment Approaches.* Washington, D.C.: National Institutes of Health, grant no. 15900–05–S1, 1975.

John T. Blong is president of Scott Community College and vice-chancellor for administration for the Eastern Iowa Community College District.

Adelbert J. Purga is dean of academic affairs at Scott Community College and associate vice-chancellor for education for the Eastern Iowa Community College District.

Auxiliary and service enterprises may be operated by the college, by a separate corporation formed by the college, or by a contract or lease operator. The concern of the college should be to provide appropriate levels of service at an acceptable profit.

Auxiliary and Service Enterprises

Wayne J. Stumph

"Auxiliary enterprises" is a label used in nearly every college in the United States. Closer examination reveals that individual colleges apply this label to a varied collection of activities. There are also differences in the way auxiliary enterprises are organized, managed, and financed. The first step, therefore, must be to establish a framework for this chapter.

The National Association of College Auxiliary Services (Clark, 1984) provides a very simple, straightforward definition: "Auxiliary services is that division of a college whose operations furnish a variety of goods and services for the support of the institution's educational program" (p. 1).

The National Association of College and University Business Officers (Welzenbach, 1982) provides a description in the chapter on auxiliary enterprises and other services in its national business manual: "An auxiliary enterprise furnishes a service directly or indirectly to students, faculty, or staff, and charges a fee related to, but not necessarily equal to, the cost of services" (p. 197).

I prefer to describe (1) what is possible and (2) what is happening in practice in various places. Each college obviously will

D. Campbell (Ed.). *Strengthening Financial Management.* New Directions for Community Colleges, no. 50. San Francisco: Jossey-Bass, June 1985.

adopt the organizational structure, operating policies, practices, labels, and definitions considered reasonable and necessary for its own campus.

A Working Definition

Auxiliary enterprises, as discussed here, are satellite business operations organized and operated by a community college for the benefit and convenience of academic departments, administrative units, staff, students, and other patrons of, or visitors to, the campus. This broad definition allows the individual college to organize a wide range of activities as auxiliary enterprises, charging the users or patrons for the goods or services supplied.

Colleges use fund-accounting practices to maintain the separation and integrity of monies that are collected and budgeted for specific purposes. A separate fund group for the collections and disbursements of auxiliary enterprises facilitates the whole process of charging operating costs appropriately to academic and operating units. As these units purchase products and services from the auxiliary enterprises, the transaction is recorded as a sale.

Within this broad framework, all manner of noneducational services may be organized as auxiliary enterprises. The most commonly found auxiliary enterprises are bookstores and food services. Food services may range from a row of vending machines to a four-star dining room operated in conjunction with a restaurant management program.

Coin-operated vending machines, game machines, copying machines, lockers, and business machines are frequently found auxiliaries, as are daycare centers, printing and graphics shops, and branch post offices. This list is far from complete; in some places, we might find bowling alleys, swimming pools, beauty and barber shops, bars, bicycle rentals, and riding stables operated as auxiliaries. A community college, though usually considered to be a commuter college, frequently has inquiries about housing and may wish to open a trailer court on campus land. Larger colleges may open travel agencies; and, in states where gambling is legal, it is even conceivable that a community college could establish an auxiliary to operate gambling machines. If the college owns aircraft and offers flight instruction, airplane rentals may be handled as auxiliaries; and if bicycles, horses, and airplanes are possible, we should not rule out automobile and truck rental.

Departments that provide specialized services to the campus, such as office machine repair and rental, maintenance, cleaning, security, photo service, and communication, are usually organized as administrative units or service departments, but they can be organized and financed as auxiliaries if the college chooses.

The chief distinction among administrative units, service departments, and auxiliary enterprises is in the source of revenue or the method of financing the unit. An administrative unit is usually financed by an allocation from the general fund budget and makes no charges for its services.

A service department, on the other hand, is often set up originally from general funds and may continue to receive budget allocations for a part of its support. It usually charges other departments for the products and/or services it provides, but a service department seldom, if ever, sells services for cash to individuals in the college community.

An auxiliary enterprise sells products and services to individuals and charges departments for services and products through interdepartment transfers. An auxiliary enterprise should be self-supporting. Start-up costs should be borrowed from other funds and repaid from operations.

Operation of Auxiliary Enterprises

The activities that we have described as auxiliary enterprises are very similar to retail businesses. The successful retail business satisfies its customers, advertises, and controls its inventories, cash, and costs. It also takes risks, adjusts to correct errors as promptly as they are identified, and invests to grow and improve. These same steps will create successful auxiliary enterprises. With a captive clientele, auxiliaries can usually survive and grow without doing all of the things that a successful retail business must do. Today, auxiliary enterprises are a multimillion-dollar operation on the campuses of medium-size community colleges. Colleges need to organize auxiliaries for success in terms of student and staff satisfaction, financial return, and growth or cutbacks that keep pace with changes in the size of the campus.

The organization of community colleges as regards auxiliary services is not consistent. The units that are described in this chapter usually report to a business services officer, but they may be a part of student services, academic affairs, or central administration, or they may be entirely separated from the college as a corporate entity or as part of a foundation. Probably the most common situation is that a variety of these units are present on campus, some organized as service departments or administrative units and possibly reporting through several administrative lines.

Ideally, auxiliaries should be collected under one officer, preferably someone with a retail management background and orientation. In a million-dollar-a-year business, 5 percent of revenue allotted for administrative overhead will provide a sufficient budget for a general manager to oversee all auxiliary enterprises.

An auxiliary organization reporting to an academic or student services division may have a customer satisfaction orientation but may lack the management direction and control to achieve its objectives and secure the best financial return possible. An auxiliary organization reporting to a business officer may suffer neglect if the more urgent demands of other responsibilities, such as budget, accounting deadlines, personnel, plant, security, and purchasing, have to be given prior attention. It is also true that a college business officer seldom has the retail background and orientation to provide the best management for auxiliaries.

A good auxiliary manager will produce a high level of service, creative additions to campus life, and return more than enough added dollar volume to pay the cost of the manager's office.

Auxiliary operations, when separated entirely from the college entity, are free from operating and financial restrictions that may be imposed by law and personnel regulations that are attuned to the academic rather than the business world. When college auxiliaries reach an annual sales volume of a million dollars or more, or have the potential to do so, the college should consider the advantages and disadvantages of placing auxiliaries under a foundation or separate corporate structure.

Whether auxiliaries are operated as a part of the college or as separate entities, policy guidelines are important to their success and should be formulated by appropriate administrators and approved by the college trustees.

Policies for auxiliaries should include, but not necessarily be limited to, pricing and profit objectives, service standards, policies for the disposition of earned surplus or subsidization of deficits, restrictions on types of businesses permissible, and product lines to be carried. Policy guidelines should also address the matter of competition with local trade.

Management

Competent management is an essential ingredient to success in any business. Not only should auxiliaries have a competent general manager for the entire group but they also need strong department managers to operate bookstores, dining rooms, print shops, and rental units. Excellent training workshops are available through the National Association of College Auxiliary Services, the National Association of College Stores, and the National Association of College Food Services. Good managers need support, refresher education, incentive, and sufficient authority to conduct the day-to-day affairs of the enterprise. The manager should be an important member of the long-range planning team for the enterprise that is the manager's responsibility.

In commercial businesses, owners learn that accounting controls must be instituted to protect their cash, inventories, and other assets from theft, shoplifting, and employee dishonesty. Colleges may be slow to implement controls. The responsible administrators do not have a personal stake in the assets of the enterprise and may feel a degree of distaste for procedures designed to check and verify financial transactions. In fact, accounting controls not only limit temptation and discover problems early but also provide a protection to the employee. Good accounting controls minimize or eliminate the possibility that an employee might be accused falsely of being responsible for shortages. Auxiliary enterprise managers owe the assurance of good controls to each employee given responsiblity for cash or inventory.

Service Departments

Service departments, as we have mentioned, are college units, such as general stores, maintenance service, printing service, photo service, and official laboratory machine repair, that exist to provide specialized service to the academic and administrative units of the college. The cost of services rendered by service departments is usually billed to the user department. Such billings should be measured carefully to reflect all appropriate costs incurred—both the direct and the variable indirect costs.

The cost of service departments, as well as the quality and convenience of their services, should be measured periodically against the cost of purchasing the service from the nearby business community.

A service department becomes an auxiliary enterprise when its services are extended to students, staff, and campus visitors on a charge basis. For example, a transportation service department would become an auxiliary enterprise if it began offering oil changes and lubrications to students and staff at commercial rates.

Other Revenue-Producing Units

Campus educational activities often make direct charges to the public and collect cash. These include admission charges for athletic, dramatic, and musical performances, clinical services, and sale of goods and services produced during instructional activity. In these activities, educational objectives are far more important than the convenience factor or potential for cost recovery or profit. Such activities will be conducted regardless of the sales or charge potential, and they should be managed by instructional or coaching staff. Auxiliary enterprise units may assist with such activities by selling tickets or products in the bookstore, buying agricultural products for use in food service units, or cooperating to provide joint services.

The Decision to Lease or Self-Operate

Auxiliary and service enterprises may be operated by the college, by a separate corporation formed by the college, or by a contract or lease operator engaged by the college to operate the enterprise. The concern of the college should be to provide appropriate levels of service and convenience, and to maximize efficient and financial advantage from auxiliary and service enterprises.

In deciding the appropriate organization and method of operation, the college should consider these factors:

- The importance of auxiliary revenue to the overall college budget
- The priorities assigned to the time of the college administrators—The college must realistically assess the administrative time available and its most effective use.
- The size and growth potential of each existing or contemplated auxiliary—Small size and small market potential seldom produce business success.
- The availability of viable lease or contract alternatives— Experienced lease operators may not be interested in small campuses or remote places.
- The ability to attract and retain experienced and competent management under existing college personnel policy limitations.
- The present level of service, profit, inventory, and management conditions in each auxiliary unit and any corrections that may be necessary.

The Future of Auxiliary Enterprises

Community colleges must face the question: "What are we doing in the retail business?" Certainly, retail business is not a primary purpose of a community college. The historic answer has been: "to provide a necessary service and convenience to students, staff, and visitors." An additional incentive has been to provide opportunities for student employment on campus.

In addition to the traditional reasons, we now find that properly planned and managed auxiliary enterprises can produce substantial revenue, as well as service, convenience, and student employment. Many colleges, unable to obtain enough support from student charges, government appropriations, gifts, and grants to maintain and improve the quality of educational services, are turning to auxiliary enterprises for their profit potential.

In the wisdom of the ancient injunction that "whatever is worth doing is worth doing well," community colleges will provide more and better auxiliary enterprises as the colleges mature and develop to their full potential.

References

Clark, S. Personal correspondence with the author, Oct. 1984.

Welzenbach, L. F. (Ed.). *College and University Business Administration.* 4th ed. Washington, D.C.: National Association of College and University Business Officers, 1982.

Wayne J. Stumph was dean of business services, Reading Area Community College in Reading, Pennsylvania.

Fiscal stringencies have added an entrepreneurial
function to the business officer's job responsibilities.
Besides funds management, administrators have new
roles in grants and contracts management and in the
solicitation of private and corporate donations.

Strategies for Generating
New Financial Resources

Bernard J. Luskin
Ida K. Warren

Fund raising at the community college has come a long way. Hard economic times, changing social priorities, and new, costly technologies have made college development a top administrative priority. Today, and in the future, the best development people will be those who are members of a management team. After all, a good development program is the job of a lot of people, and, while it is stretching things to say that development is everyone's job, certainly all of the key people in any institution need to be involved.

This chapter discusses the team approach to college development and examines the role of grants and contracts, foundations, business and industry donations, alumni associations, and planned giving efforts in community college financial resource development.

The Team Approach

The Development Office Team. A successful chief development officer is a builder of effective teams, beginning with his or her own

D. Campbell (Ed.). *Strengthening Financial Management.* New Directions for
Community Colleges, no. 50. San Francisco: Jossey-Bass, June 1985.

staff. Team spirit is fostered by the development officer's vision of achieving a balanced program that offers a broad spectrum of opportunities to a potential donor. The development person knows that the plan that offers maximum benefits for all parties offers the greatest sense of satisfaction for the donor and the most benefits for the institution.

But how does a development officer go about implementing this vision? He or she puts all possibilities in perspective by using a priority list that is intended to reflect institutional policy. This list, although only for internal use, will remind staff members that all gifts are desirable and necessary. Some gifts benefit the institution sooner, but, if the circumstances of the donor dictate using one form of gift over another, each gift should be greeted with equal enthusiasm and appreciation by the development team.

No one questions that an outright gift is the most desirable. But if a donor cannot make an outright gift, a pledge that is payable over three to five years and can be spent when received is a welcome gift. If those two forms are impossible to achieve, why not suggest a gift annuity or a charitable remainder trust? Finally, there is the bequest by will.

The initiation of a priority list will enable all development staff members to keep in mind the importance of each gift. No one form of giving should be urged on donors when it is not in their best interests or because the development staff member has a specialty and can't resist using it.

Role of the Business Office. If an institution has a development office, that office must reach out to other institutional areas for team support. Although marketing and administrative plans begin in the development office, the business office immediately becomes involved with the operation of them, and the development policy and operating procedures must define clearly the role and responsibilities of the business office in trust management, investment decisions, and program accounting. Routine matters, such as sending tax reports and trust reports to donors and mailing checks on time so that donors know which gift prompted payment, affect the attitude of donors as well as the possibility of future gifts. Every transaction must reflect accuracy, promptness, and courtesy. It is not an easy job, but it is crucial to all development endeavors.

The Solicitation Team. The successful development operation builds effective solicitation teams composed of institutional leaders and powerful friends. A recent survey conducted by the Council for Advancement and Support of Education (CASE) (Winship, 1984) sheds light on the composition of these solicitation teams and the relative effectiveness of each category of leadership. The survey points to the importance of institutional leaders to development efforts and notes that, "notorious though many of our presidents are for their disclaimers of fund-raising prowess, most institutions look to them to take the lead, and apparently they are doing so—successfully. This may be nothing new, but the affirmation is welcome" (p. 5).

Likewise, chief development officers and their senior development associates are effective solitation team members, and so are volunteers. Volunteerism has been described as diminishing, but the CASE survey suggests differently: "There may be a reordering of the respective roles, with professional staff moving more prominently into front-line positions, but there is no general sense of less volunteerism" (Winship, 1984, p. 5).

A development program has only a small probability of success without team skill building—first on the level of the core office, then on the institutional management level, and finally on the presidential and governing board level. A full commitment is needed to maximize all efforts in this direction. An institution must want a development program, not fear it. The institution must make a short-term investment of adequate money to ensure a successful program that will in turn produce assets and enable the leadership to plan for the future with confidence. However the effort is structured, it must be well thought out and have an institutional priority.

Establishing a College Foundation

According to Sharron (1978), there are two purposes for establishing a community college foundation: "to provide an alternative vehicle for contribution of funds to support activities and programs at the institution that are not adequately being funded through traditional resources . . . [and] for public relations" (p. 2).

As has been pointed out by Kopecek (1980), the creation of a foundation offers an advantage both to the donor and to the institution. Since foundations can be incorporated under state law so as to qualify for federal tax-exempt status, donors who contribute to a foundation receive a tax deduction, whereas the same donor, if he or she were to give directly to a public college, would not receive a tax benefit. This tax benefit creates an incentive for the donor and a benefit to the community college in the form of increased giving, which, in turn, enables special projects to be conducted with the monies donated to the foundation.

Of course, steps in the development of a foundation will vary from state to state, but according to Sharron (1978), who studied 1,037 public community colleges, there are four general phases of development through which all successful community college foundations evolve. This process generally takes from nine to twelve months to complete, and each step is crucial to success. The four phases are: (1) organizational and administrative period; (2) educational awareness period; (3) community relations period; (4) planning and implementation period.

Phase one is comprised of six distinct activities: establishing a foundation committee; discussing foundation models; reviewing concepts; identifying contact persons; presenting proposals to the trustees; and garnering board sanction. The process of starting up is critical. The foundation first needs friends and a special focus. The role of the foundation must be distinguished and assigned an exclusive area of programming with which potential contributors can readily identify. A pattern of such program activities has emerged that has proven to be made up of good "starter" projects: scholarships; faculty development; cultural programs; and matching money.

The second phase, development and organization, consists of three major activities: the identification of board members; the development of brochures; and the preparation of a multimedia presentation. Both the brochures and the multimedia presentation must be made brief and specific to the foundation in order to be effective.

The selection of the foundation board and its composition will make or break the foundation. The selection process must be conducted in such a way that the entire college feels ownership in the foundation. Some colleges have asked faculty and staff to nominate board members. This accomplishes two things: It lets everyone know that a foundation is being established, and it sends out the message that the foundation will serve the entire institution. It is also important to separate the foundation board from the board of trustees. Trustees are picked to act as administrators, whereas foundation board members are picked to act as fund raisers and should be chosen as such.

After the foundation board is selected, very careful attention must be paid to the first meeting. To get the first board meeting off to a good start, the college may need to hire consultants. Consultants can help clarify the roles of the board members, and, as outsiders, they can say things that institutional leaders might find awkward to say. The consultants can also help determine a realistic plan of action and an attendant timetable that ensures the success of the first venture.

Phase three begins the administrative cycle. Typically, the foundation board has a kickoff dinner and presentation. The meeting following the event is used for the election of officers and the identification of other potential board members if the board is not totally filled. At this time, the board ratifies its articles and bylaws so that they may be formally filed, along with tax-exempt status papers. The board is then ready to turn to the business of the foundation.

Phase four consists of planning and implementation. During this time, the board busies itself with the setting of priorities, again looking for special-focus projects and ordering them so as to reflect the college's financing plans and priorities. By this time, the first year is almost over, and it is time to implement the plans for the second year. This ushers in the last planning phase—that of community relations. The special program priorities must be well publicized through a hard-hitting publicity campaign. Personal contacts must also be expanded to find friends of the institution who are also community leaders willing to volunteer services to work on one special project. Once persons who are recognized leaders show their support, it becomes "the thing to do" and others quickly follow suit.

The foundation is now launched and its success will depend upon the commitment of the chief executive officer, the work of the board, and the appropriateness of the foundation's goals for general public support.

Alumni Associations

Although most community colleges have not yet formed an alumni association, alumni are of increasing interest to community colleges because they can add to the financial support base of the college and enhance the college's public image.

Dr. Isaac Beckes (1984), a president of Vincennes University (Indiana), pioneered the development of community college alumni associations. In 1958, an alumni office was opened at Vincennes as part of the Office of Public Relations. Later the Office of Alumni Programs was established and a full-time director was hired. When the college established its foundation, the Office of Alumni Programs was moved organizationally, and the alumni director reported directly to the director of the foundation. This office has worked so well for Vincennes that today three alumni chapters have been established.

Recently, a planning group was formed consisting of past student body officials. The group met to determine ways to promote the college and to provide a mechanism for former students to participate in college activities. From the beginning, Beckes has stressed the importance of graduates' aid to the college. Alumni can:

- Help to interpret and improve the college's mission
- Assist with the recruitment of students and help increase enrollment in academic transfer programs
- Assist in tracking alumni
- Help to improve curricular offerings by suggesting new programs
- Become involved in the college's activities
- Help organize alumni chapters throughout the state
- Provide financial assistance.

These seven areas could serve as a basic set of activities for any alumni group.

Alumni programs offer a means for graduates to be helpful to their alma mater as they pursue their goals and progress in their careers. The next ten years will be challenging ones for community colleges. Alumni can help us meet this challenge.

Planned Giving

William B. Dunseth (1978) recently reported to CASE members that, in just twenty years, planned or deferred giving has moved from a somewhat hazy concept to a formalized program. Yet Dunseth found that only 30 percent of institutions surveyed by the Council for Financial Aid to Education (CFAE) reported full programs covering life-income gifts and annuity programs. This is the area of the future in development work and institutional financing. In fact, there is evidence based on recent capital campaigns that a very high proportion—sometimes as much as 75 to 80 percent—of new endowment monies has come through annuity and life-income programs and bequests. This means that no chief development officer has the luxury of neglecting this area.

Yet such a program is not the responsibility solely of the chief development officer. A program of planned giving has only a small chance of success without the commitment of the institution's president and board members. As in other segments of a development program, the solicitation of annuities and charitable trusts will be most effective when carried out according to policies and guidelines adopted by the governing board and the president, and with adequate time and budget. It takes time and attention to develop an understanding of the various plans, the obligations, and responsibilities of the institution. It is unfair to judge the success of any development program in less than three years. In addition to a need for competent staff, the college should be willing to spend monies in this as in other development areas to "send personnel to conferences, hire professional counsel, and spend considerable amounts on brochures, mailings, luncheons, banquets, cocktail parties, and meetings to plan and carry out the program. . . . Fitting the plan to the donor takes expertise and time. An unskilled person cannot do it" (Dunseth, 1978, p. 21).

Benefits. All planned giving programs have four common characteristics: (1) the gifts are irrevocable; (2) the right to use income or property is retained by the donor and/or others; (3) there are tax benefits for donors (income, capital gains, estate, and inheritance); and (4) the remaining principal at the death of the last beneficiary is available for use by the institution.

The donor receives several benefits: the opportunity to make a gift during his or her lifetime when income cannot be lost; the chance to make a larger gift than could be made as an outright gift; the ability both to make a gift and, at the same time, to reserve income for life to a beneficiary; encouragement to begin the estate-planning process; an opportunity to create a memorial to honor others; gratification of the urge to give; and tax benefits.

To the institution, there is the benefit of attracting gifts that cannot be revoked, the assurance of funds for the future, and the ability to plan for the future with some confidence since the assets are in hand. The different ways of facilitating planned giving are deferred gifts, the pooled income fund, and charitable trusts.

Deferred Gifts. A donor may be able to claim a substantial deduction for a gift that will not be received by the institution until some time in the future. This is accomplished by using a pooled income fund or an annuity trust or a unitrust. When cash, securities, or real property are made contributions, the donor continues to receive the income—usually for his or her lifetime plus the lifetime of his or her spouse. At the end of the time, the property belongs to the institution. The tax benefit, though, is not deferred but begins immediately for the donor. The donor takes the deduction in the year the contribution is made for the value of the property less the value of the expected income. The amount of deduction can be determined from tables based upon life expectancy and expected investment yield.

Pooled Income Fund. This plan involves very little paperwork and few legal complications. A college establishes a pooled income fund. Gifts from all the donors are commingled and managed by a professional in the way that a mutual fund is managed. The donor receives a steady annual income based upon current yields and consistent with his or her share of the total assets in the fund. Thus, through the gift, the donor may be able to increase his or her annual income, eliminate potential capital gains tax, and reduce his or her estate tax. If the donor donates appreciated securities, the tax benefit will be maximized. Thus, this plan has a lot to offer to the potential donor, and it should be very easy for the development team to "sell."

Charitable Remainder Annuity Trusts and Unitrusts. These trusts work in much the same way as pooled income funds. There are two major differences, however. First, the trust is created by the donor, and its assets consist only of the funds or property the donor contributes. Second, the donor sets the amount of income to be received rather than receiving a prorated share, as a donor would in the case of a pooled income fund. This allows the donor to design an arrangement that meets his or her financial needs. Additionally, these trusts allow more flexibility in the types of property that can be donated. Municipal bonds may also be used so that the donor can receive tax-free income.

Under an annuity trust, the beneficiary receives a fixed dollar amount each year, but that amount cannot be less than 5 percent of the original value of the trust assets when the trust was created. The unitrust is set up so that a beneficiary receives a fixed percentage (no less than 5 percent of each year of the value of the assets held in trust). For further discussion of annuity trusts versus unitrusts, see Cooper and Lybrand (1984, p. 3).

Evaluating a Planned Giving Program. The Lilly Endowment financed a two-year study to determine the relationship of cost to benefits for an institution of a planned giving program, and some general tenets were established. One is that each institution must refine its own plan and set its own criteria for minimum ages and amounts. Where these differ, results are not comparable. Second, the longer a college must manage an agreement and/or the higher the payout, the lower the benefit to the college. Third, personal solicitation works better than a mail campaign. Fourth, donors who are strangers to the college will give for the tax benefit. Fifth, the director of such a program should have special expertise. In sum, each institution will have its own criteria, monitor its program, and make decisions that are in its best interest. These programs are the fastest growing sources of income for institutions and represent yet another way an institution may offer donors a choice of giving best suited to their circumstances and objectives.

Corporate Giving

Probably the most elusive area of fund raising is corporate giving. The Filer Commission, with all its power and prestige, did not deal with it except to say that it was "unimpressive and inadequate" and to urge corporations to increase their giving to 2 percent of their profits (they are currently giving just below 1 percent). Yet the truth is, someone is giving away corporate money ($3.1 billion a year), and someone is getting it despite the rhetoric to the contrary.

If you ask a corporate executive how to approach a corporation, he or she will probably say to approach the corporation confidently, but first do your homework—get to know the corporation: the personalities, the corporation's interests, its programs and goals. The executive will then probably say that the interests of the stockholders govern contributions. This, of course, is good advice, but there are nagging inconsistencies of which a chief development officer must be aware. Shakely (1983) of the Grantsmanship Center gives the clearest elucidation of the problem:

> For those corporations that have stockholders, let's look at how they work. Cities Service Corporation, the oil company, has over 135,000 stockholders, yet fewer than 150 showed up for the last annual stockholders' meeting. This pattern is not unusual at all. . . . The SEC does not require any philanthropic information in the annual report to stockholders, so the vast majority don't know where, or if, the corporation is giving. *Corporations are controlled by management, pure and simple.* (p. 47).

To understand what a corporation believes, then, one needs to know what its management believes. A good source of information is *Who's Who* and *Who Was Who.* Both give brief biographical information on many corporate leaders; the data provided include awards, offices, boards, and other community ties. It is also a good idea to check with local chambers of commerce, which publish directories of local corporations. Finally, if a corporation has a foundation, it must publish a form detailing every grant made by the corporation (published in *Corporate Foundation Profiles*). (It is important to keep in mind, however, that a corporation is just as likely to give directly, in which case nothing may appear in that publication.)

Because corporate giving tends to be local in scope, a personal approach usually works better than it does with large foundations. Yet this can be both a strength and a weakness. The access to a corporate leader is high, but not everyone has developed the skill needed in the approach. Although the development officer may intend the first meeting with the corporate executive to be just an "information sharing," and although both may have agreed to this, one must be prepared to make a full presentation, as there may not be a second chance. Corporate executive officers (CEOs) pride themselves on making quick decisions, and there is a good chance that the CEO will decide at the initial meeting whether to give or not. One secret is to bring a friend along who has some personal or peer relationship with the CEO. It is even more important to be accompanied by a local peer when contacting a CEO who is halfway across the country.

When meeting the CEO, keep in mind the ten rules proposed by the Grantsmanship Center:

1. Make sure that you have some information about the person with whom you are meeting.

2. Never go with a prepared text in your head; you must listen with extreme care to the person you are meeting in order to decide in which direction you should move.

3. Have notes jotted on a note pad in front of you so that he or she knows you are prepared.

4. Most individuals of stature do not like long meetings, so get to the point once you have determined the directions you need to take.

5. If you are with others, observe protocol in addressing the person; even if you are on a first-name basis, conduct yourself in a formal manner. In private, be formal until he or she makes a point of letting you know that that isn't necessary.

6. Most people feel that your dress is a reflection of your attitude toward them. It is therefore extremely important to dress meticulously for these sessions. Dress is also a measure of success. No one likes to become involved with someone who does not appear successful.

7. Be aggressive (but not obnoxious or overbearing), even if it destroys your insides.

8. Prominent people will want to help if you are sincere and reasonable.

9. Be honest. If prominent individuals find you have misled them, you will lose not only their respect but also that of other individuals with whom they are in contact.

10. Read a good book on how to be a lobbyist.

There are five basic areas of support from corporations that a development officer should consider. Each is discussed in the following subsections.

Outright Gifts and Grants. Outright gifts from corporations tend to be smaller than those from foundations. If the corporation does not have a foundation, it tends to give through program grants. Many corporations, including some of the largest, tend to give geographically, based on the percentage of workers in the area.

The following are four common types of outright gifts from corporations:

1. *The check out the door*—These are small grants—$100, for example, to purchase tickets—for a worthy cause.

2. *General support contributions*—These are gifts made to agencies and institutions more out of overall respect than for a project. Most corporate gifts to higher education are of this type. According to the Grantsmanship Center, new or less established institutions may find these difficult to secure unless a direct link between the company and the institution can be made.

3. *Programmatic grants*—These are grants for specific projects addressing specific problems. This is the type of gift that corporations that have defined objectives prefer.

4. *Corporate-sponsored projects*—These are projects that the company initiates and carries out by having an agency or institution deliver the project services.

Matching Grants. The fastest growing area of corporate support is that of matching grants. Some corporations are now extending matching gifts to art groups, hospitals, and the public media. Some companies match dollar for dollar up to a set amount, while others, like Exxon, match three to one. This is popular both because it is seen as an employee benefit and because it fosters good will for the corporation. Almost 700 corporations now have some form of matching gifts contributions program.

Volunteerism. Another form of contribution comes from released staff time or volunteerism. The Filer Commission reported that 92 percent of CEOs said they did philanthropic work during company hours. Some spent as much as five hours per week. There are three major models of support of this kind:

1. *The company incentive program* is a program whereby the company will support community organizations in which a company employee is a volunteer. To get funds, the employee must write the

request, describe the project, and name the amount requested. Ninety percent of all employee requests are granted, according to the Grantsmanship Center.

2. *The loaned executive program* is a second model. Under this program, an employee receives release time to work full-time for a nonprofit organization for periods up to a full year. The corporation pays the loaned executive's salary.

3. *The corporate volunteer program* is a model where corporate-wide volunteering focuses all employee volunteer efforts on one program area chosen by the corporation.

In-Kind Gifts. In an in-kind gifts program, a corporation donates an inventory item rather than declaring an inventory loss. In order for the corporation to take this deduction, the receiving institution must write a letter to the corporation certifying its nonprofit status and stating that the item will not be resold.

Pooled Corporate Trust. The pooled corporate trust is a recent innovation. Under this arrangement, an institution needing money to conduct a three-year project may find more acceptance from corporations through the trust. Let us say ten corporations agree to loan an educational institution $200,000 each for three years, equaling a pooled trust of two million dollars. The institution keeps the money in trust, using the interest received, say $200,000 a year, to conduct the project. At the end of the third year, each corporation receives back the amount it pooled.

Summary

There are many approaches available to community colleges in generating new financial resources. Seeking grants and contracts is the most common. More than 300 federal categorical program titles are accessible to community colleges, yet most colleges only deal with the well-known dozen. Project development for these programs requires constant effort, but it can pay significant dividends. Unsolicited contracts are less common but offer a fertile new source of funds.

Foundations are new but are becoming more common, and techniques in using foundations are worth sharing among ourselves.

Business and industry donations constitute another new and growing area, and, while the technique and viability of using alumni associations to generate funds has yet to emerge, there are a few of these organizations around the nation that show promise.

Industry contracting is another developing resource, and we

will be reading more about this area in the literature in the near future.

Money moves people and people move programs. Development is important to the viability of college programs because of the impact of funds on the institution and ultimately the students—and, I suppose, a basic question underlying the issue of new resources in times of declining funds is "where's the buck?"

References

Beckes, I. K. Personal Communication, January 10, 1984.

Cooper and Lybrand. *Guide to Charitable Giving: Colleges and Universities*. Washington, D.C. 1984.

Dunseth, W. B. *An Introduction to Annuity, Charitable Remainder Trusts, and Bequests Programs*. Washington, D.C.: Council for Advancement and Support of Education, 1978.

Kopecek, R. J. *The Alumni—An Untapped Reservoir of Support*. Paper presented at the conference of the National Council on Community Services and Continuing Education, Madison, Wisconsin, October, 1980.

Shakely, J. "Researching Corporate Giving." *Grantsmanship Center News,* Rosedale, Calif., 1983.

Sharron, W. H., Jr. *The Development and Organization of the Community College Foundation*. Resources Paper no. 18. Washington, D.C.: National Council for Resource Development, 1978.

Winship, A. L., II. *The Quest for Major Gifts: A Survey of Sixty-Eight Institutions*. Washington, D.C.: Council for Advancement and Support of Education, 1984.

Bernard J. Luskin is executive vice-president of the American Association of Community and Junior Colleges.

Ida K. Warren is director of development of the American Association of Community and Junior Colleges.

*Every institution, regardless of size, deserves mature
financial management. Somewhere amid the purchase
orders, budget printouts, and campus traffic tickets, there
must be help for the campus business officer as she or he
wears the investment manager's hat.*

Managing and Investing
College Funds

Charles E. Taylor, Jr.
Dennis Greenway

One way to gauge the financial maturity of an educational institution
is to evaluate its endowment and reserves. Some large universities and
old-guard private colleges have been successful in achieving that
maturity.

Younger institutions, many community colleges among them,
may not yet have obtained that financial maturity measured by huge
endowments and impressive reserves. There is good reason to hope,
however. Many of the younger, more aggressive colleges are finding
that their successes are not going unnoticed by benefactors who, in the
past, may have limited their giving to those institutions with ivy-
covered walls. Institutions are gearing up development efforts to glean
their "fair share" of gift and grant income from foundations, private
donors, and alumni. The rising star at many financially immature
institutions may well be the aggressive development officer who can
open doors to resources heretofore closed.

As if getting the resources is not hard enough, institutions had
also better be prepared to do something with what they get. It has been
said that experience is the best teacher, but this does present a

D. Campbell (Ed.). *Strengthening Financial Management.* New Directions for
Community Colleges, no. 50. San Francisco: Jossey-Bass, June 1985.

problem. Experience always gives the exam before it teaches the lesson. During the 1970s, inflation and high interest rates taught many colleges some valuable lessons. Some took those lessons with them to the grave. Endowment and reserves sitting idle or poorly invested were ravaged by double-digit inflation. The lesson is a simple one. An endowment dollar in hand today may not buy a dollar's worth of endowment benefit tomorrow unless it is prudently managed.

Couched in more positive terms, this lesson teaches that there is great opportunity for the well-managed fund to appreciate beyond the point of inflation. In fact, it can provide the college with still another source of increased resources. This possibility should be incentive enough to master a few ground rules of investment management.

The size of the numbers notwithstanding, every institution deserves mature financial management—management that takes seriously its stewardship of the funds in its charge. While financially mature institutions can afford to hire specialists to manage their assets, there are many other colleges that must rely on that old reliable business officer (title him or her what you will) for leadership in investment management. Somewhere amid those purchase orders, budget printouts, and campus traffic tickets, there must be help for the business management generalist when he or she must wear the investment manager's hat.

Stating Investment Objectives

One of the more valuable tools for the investment manager is a document that we will refer to as the statement of investment objectives. Almost any name that identifies the document as an investment policy statement will suffice. Its true value is not in the name, the form, or even the complete accuracy of its contents. The document's real value lies in the mental discipline required to produce it. It is the process of producing such a statement that provides the framework for writing this chapter.

It is appropriate to limit this consideration of investments to those funds that we know as endowments. Some definition of terms is in order. There are three categories of endowment funds, each having as a common characteristic the restriction that the principal is only expendable under certain conditions. *Term endowment* funds are funds for which the donor has stipulated that the principal may be expended after a stated period or on the occurrence of a certain event. *True endowment* funds are funds received from a donor with the restriction that the principal is not expendable in perpetuity. A *quasi-endowment* is a fund that is established by the governing board to function like an endowment fund but that may be totally expended at any time at the discretion of the governing board. (Welzenbach, 1982).

While the principal of an endowment must remain intact, the income earned is available for use. This principal-income distinction is important to the investor since he or she must provide for adequate income to satisfy the purposes of the funds and hopefully to produce some increase or appreciation of the principal itself. Whether one holds to the conventional concept that the endowment is a trust or whether the more liberal view is taken that some of the appreciation may be used prudently, maintenance of and appreciation of the principal is central.

In beginning with the statement of objectives, we assume that those involved in the management of investments for the college are properly empowered by existing law and the required action of the governing board. Typically, the business officer will be assisted in this role by an investment committee of the board of trustees. Approval of the finalized statement of objectives and guidelines should rest with this committee as a minimum. It may be desirable to get the full board's endorsement, since the investment management objectives must complement the goals of the college as a whole.

A good beginning for the document is a general goals statement. You should refer to the purposes for which the funds exist and to how the proper management of the funds will enhance the chances that those purposes will continue to be achieved. This is the place to insert the part about maintenance of and perhaps improvement of the funds' purchasing power. Because the final document will be used as an assessment tool, it is important to go beyond generalizations. It is easy to say that the college wants to maximize its long-term total return on investments, but it is not as easy to quantify that kind of language with a statement like "the college's investment management goal is to earn a cumulative 4 percent annual return above the annualized rate of inflation as measured by the Higher Education Pricing index." There will be years when such objectives will be easy to formulate. But, in times of economic uncertainty, such as the seventies, objectives will be more difficult to specify. It is important to make this document something the college can live with in the long term.

Another necessary element of the general goals statement is the college's position on the amount of risk that is acceptable in an effort to maximize return. Can the college afford a negative return on investment and, if so, how much in any given year—5 percent, 10 percent? You also need to mention that the college will have current income needs to be met from these invested funds. These needs must also be quantified, although not specifically in this document. A statement such as "the funds are to be managed such that sufficient current return is available to satisfy the budgeted needs from the funds" will be sufficient. This approach allows the percentage of income required to vary from budget year to budget year without altering the objectives and guidelines statement (Williams, 1980).

This yearly assessment of budget needs should not be taken lightly. Perhaps as much as any single factor, this figure will set the tone of the college's investment program. An example best explains the reason. In a time of appreciating stock market prices, the college defines its needs for endowment income at 10 percent when it only needs 6 percent. In order to achieve the 10 percent income return, investors are forced to choose from a limited number of high-interest bonds and some cash equivalents. The result is often forfeiture of the opportunity to participate in a stock market that could yield sizable appreciation for the fund but could not meet the income require-ments. Another scenario can be constructed such that an underestimation of the college's needs results in too little income to meet current needs. The point is simply that income needs should be well documented because of their direct impact upon investment strategy.

Success is a relative term, and investment results are no exception. Since accountability is one of the recurring themes in this volume, it is necessary to establish some benchmarks against which performance can be judged. This task can be as simple or as complex as the situation demands. Use of the Standard and Poors 500 Stock Index and the Salomon Brothers Bond Index may be appropriate. The consolidated performance records of other endowment funds are another possibility. The more sophisticated tools use a measure of the amount of risk taken for purposes of comparison. Other funds incorporate time weighting and dollar weighting to improve accuracy. The latter measurements tend to be difficult to obtain and expensive as well. Regardless of the approach, the use of some performance measurement device is important.

Investment Restrictions

After defining the goals for an endowment fund investment program, you need to establish some boundaries within which the program can be operated. The first such restriction should be the definition of the acceptable range of investments.

Equities. Equities (ownership rights in other entities) should be included but not without some further restrictions. Among these restrictions are:

1. Acceptable categories—Common and preferred stocks may be foregone conclusions, but what about warrants, options, and so on?

2. Marketability—It is good to exclude private placements, restricted stocks, and public issues with limited market appeal. A statement restricting most or all of the fund's holdings to those stocks traded on major exchanges may be in order.

3. Size of holdings—Investors should not be permitted to concentrate stock holdings in one company for at least two reasons. Large holdings restrict marketability. Too many shares expose the fund to pressures associated with the company's internal management. A restriction of holdings to not more than 5 percent of the fund's assets in the stock of any one company may avoid these problems. Diversification is also recommended among industry groups within the portfolio. Some maximum concentration of the fund's assets in any one industry group is recommended.

4. Social acceptability—It may be appropriate to restrict investment in companies whose dealings are inconsistent with the moral or social positions of the college. Care should be exercised to see that this provision does not become a political hot potato. With the advent of conglomerates, it has become very difficult to discern who owns what kind of business. This can be handled with a general statement that the desire of the governing board is to hold securities in only those companies whose business activities are consistent with the stated moral and social values of the college. The statement might be qualified to allow for inadvertent violations.

Fixed-Income Securities. Fixed-income securities (loans to other entities) include bonds, notes, and so-called cash equivalents. Bonds may be mortgage debentures, subordinated or municipal. Municipal bonds serve no useful purpose for endowment funds. Subordinated issues should be scrutinized very carefully. Prudence dictates that bonds purchased be rated highly by a recognized rating service. A minimum "A" rating would be a reasonable restriction.

Cash equivalents include United States Treasury bills, certificates of deposit, commercial paper, and a host of other short-term investment opportunities including diversified money market funds (Hagg, 1977).

Notes include those of private corporations as well as those of the United States Treasury and other government agencies.

An overconcentration of investments in the debt of a single issuer is not healthy. Some limitation should be stated. Such a limitation should probably exclude securities of the government. Further restrictions on cash-equivalent investments that are not fully secured or insured should be included.

Other Investments. Traditionally, endowment investments have been limited to those outlined above. However, some colleges have ventured into other fields, such as international investments and real estate ventures. While the institution may wish to avoid these types of investments now, it would not hurt to provide for their use with the restriction that they be used only with the prior approval of the investment committee.

Without question, the statement of objectives and guidelines should contain this wording: "In no case is any investment authorized that will jeopardize the tax-exempt status of the endowment fund."

Asset Mix

Restriction of the acceptable types of investment should be followed with some guidelines addressing the appropriate mix of the assets invested. As mentioned earlier, diversification is a key to the protection of the fund's assets. To ensure that there is a balance among investments, you should define a desired range. This range is usually stated as a percentage of the total fund's assets. Caution should be exercised so that the necessary flexibility to move from one form of investment to another is not unduly hindered. This is especially true if a professional investment manager is employed. Presenting a manager with a very restricted asset mix would be like employing an architect to design a building and then presenting him or her with floor plans and an elevation drawing.

On the other hand, if the investing is done "in house" or if specialized investment managers (equity or fixed income only) are retained, more stringent asset mix limitations may be in order. In the latter instance, the asset mix will determine how much of the total endowment fund's assets will be put at the disposal of each manager.

Investment Services

It is beyond the scope of this chapter to discuss the employment of professional investment managers. However, if the investment policy statement is to be complete, it must deal with the possibility that such services might be retained. Further, the statement should establish the framework for a working relationship with any investment managers employed. Such a framework should:

- Identify the college employee who will be the liaison with the investment manager (usually this will be the business officer)
- Grant the investment manager full discretionary authority to trade securities within the limits of the guidelines
- Specify reporting requirements, both the contents and the frequency
- Clarify the question of brokerage placement. About the last of these functions, we should note that the college may retain the right to designate the brokerage firm to be used. This "soft money" is a good way to compensate brokers who may lend assistance in the establishment of an investment program. Remember, however, that this practice can limit the investment manager when he or she seeks the best price, commission rate, or service.

Finally, it should be recognized that the investment policy statement should not be cast in concrete. As the college's investment program matures, changes in the document will be needed. Such changes should only be made with the knowledge and consent of the group that initially approved it.

While every element of a good investment policy statement is not included here, the idea of formalizing your college's investment plan is a good one. The discipline required will help clarify the direction your program will take and eliminate many of the pitfalls. Hopefully, the lessons learned will not be those taught by experience. The exam will come soon enough!

References

Hagg, L. H. *Cash Management and Short-Term Investments for Colleges and Universities.* Washington, D.C.: National Association of College and University Business Officers, 1977.

Welzenbach, L. F. (Ed.). *College and University Business Administration.* 4th ed. Washington, D.C.: National Association of College and University Business Officers, 1982.

Williams, A., III. *Managing Your Investment Manager.* Homewood, Ill.: Dow Jones-Irwin, 1980.

Charles E. Taylor, Jr., is vice president for business and finance at Meredith College in Raleigh, North Carolina.

Dennis Greenway is vice president and financial consultant for Robinson-Humphrey/American Express, Inc.

Part 3.
Emerging Issues and Implications

Professional development of the financial administrator in public policy analysis is a small cost to pay for improved capacity in strategic management.

Emerging Issues in Public Policy and Financial Administration

Richard L. Alfred

Financial administrators in community colleges are divided between strategic and operational management and the realization that resource allocation decisions are only as good as the strategy upon which decisions of this type are based. Administrators hope that the application of new information to financial decisions through techniques such as environmental scanning, program review, and zero-based budgeting will solve looming revenue and expenditure problems. However, strategic management often breaks down when problems of time, training, and limited resources drive the costs of involvement beyond the benefits. Active involvement in strategic management is further constrained by policies and regulations of federal and state agencies that command increasing time and attention on the part of financial administrators. The result is a tendency for decision makers to become accustomed to, if not comfortable with, an operational view of management.

    This chapter will advance the argument that financial administrators in community colleges must be cognizant of trends in public

D. Campbell (Ed.). *Strengthening Financial Management.* New Directions for Community Colleges, no. 50. San Francisco: Jossey-Bass, June 1985.

policy at the federal, state, and local levels if the financial strategy guiding the flow of resources to programs and services is to be effective. New mechanisms are constantly being sought to address policy issues that have a direct impact on the financial condition of community colleges. These policy issues transcend business and accounting practices commonly used to develop and maintain the operating budget. They strike at the very heart of the college—its programs, its relationships with revenue sources, and its responsiveness to changing constituency needs and expectations. To build sound fiscal strategy, financial officers will need to develop answers to the following questions, all of which involve an understanding of public policy: What is the future mission and program/service mix of the community college in a period of rapid change in demography, technology, and economic conditions? What evidence can be derived from examination of trends and conditions in American social institutions—the family, economy, government, and education—that may provide insights into programmatic emphases in tomorrow's community college? What is the relationship between public policy conditions and institutional strategic decisions, and how does this relationship shape financial strategy? What programmatic alternatives can financial decision makers pursue to position community colleges favorably for a changing public policy agenda in the late eighties?

The concepts presented in this chapter are predicated on three assumptions. First, community colleges are adaptive institutions requiring considerable slack in organizational structure and resources to provide comprehensive services to external constituencies. In the absence of slack, institutional growth will be constrained as the focus of management shifts from "development" to "maintenance." Second, organizational complexity in community colleges will continue to grow as will efforts to redefine the institutional mission, program/service mix, and financial base in response to changing external conditions. Third, pressure for new growth in enrollments and resources will mount among community college administrators and trustees as issues associated with decline—reduction, reallocation, and retrenchment—command increasing attention among groups inside and outside of the college. Although external conditions may dictate reduction, fiscal stability is still the expected norm; only continued growth and development will bring satisfaction to administrators. Stated more simply, although the conditions affecting community colleges will change dramatically in the remainder of the decade, what is expected of financial administrators will remain the same.

Paradoxes, Public Policy, and Institutional Positioning

During the past two decades, community colleges have become more diverse in the mission, programs, and services they provide as part of a strategy to increase enrollments and thereby to secure additional resources to serve even more students. The mission and programs of the college have come under increasing scrutiny by a number of constituencies who argue that the college is attempting to serve too many purposes and too many factions. This perception has signaled a new focus for public policy, shifting the emphasis from comprehensiveness to singularity in purpose, from quantity to quality, and from access to success. Implicit in this shift is a series of paradoxes that administrators in community colleges need to address if they are to align the programmatic and revenue base of the institution with emerging policy conditions. These paradoxes are the following:

- Institutional commitment to open access, yet inadequate state and local resources to fund low- or no-cost tuition policies
- The effort to expand the institutional mission to include delivery of specialized services to multiple interest groups, yet mounting pressure from state agencies to constrict the mission to "core" educational activities
- The current status of the associate degree as a credential for access to technical and paraprofessional jobs, yet transition in the labor market that could diminish the value of the degree in favor of educational preparation provided through alternative degree programs
- The historical development of community colleges as quick-response, growth-oriented institutions maintaining adequate discretionary income for new program development, yet current revenue/expenditure ratios that prohibit growth and innovation
- The requirement for institutional renewal posed by advancing technology and changing economic conditions, yet escalating costs for maintenance—energy, computing, libraries, and renovation of facilities—that could consume the full amount of resources available for renewal.

The capacity of institutions to address these paradoxes successfully depends, in part, on administrative understanding of the relationship between public policy and institutional positioning. Institutional positioning can be viewed as the interrelationship of institutional characteristics and public policy conditions to achieve the optimum competitive position for the college. Known, for example, is the fact that community colleges are positioned for enrollment growth in periods of economic recession and technological change, since they serve a large adult population requiring continuous training and retraining to remain abreast of changing labor market needs. Unknown, however, is the capacity of community colleges to adjust to changing family structures, economic conditions, and technology in a postindustrial economy. Administrators have only just begun to apply environmental scanning techniques to the decision process. They experience difficulty in distinguishing cause-and-effect relationships in the absence of baseline information about the impact of the environment on the institution. Failure to understand the linkage among institutional characteristics, environmental conditions, and the public policy initiatives of government agencies can lead to poor decisions regarding institutional positioning alternatives and to overconfidence about revenue estimates for new and continuing operations.

Emerging Public Policy Conditions

We can view public policy as a two-dimensional construct comprised of: (1) *antecedent conditions* (economic and financial conditions, social attitudes, demographic transition, changing technology, and so on) that impact complex organizations and (2) *initiatives* advanced by government agencies to maximize, alleviate, or counteract the effects of antecedent conditions. We then need to ask questions about the impact of public policy on financial administration. How do changing public policy conditions impact the flow of resources to community colleges from state and local sources? What are the antecedents to policy formation in state and local government agencies? What steps can community college financial administrators take to position the institution favorably for resource acquisition in a period of changing public policy?

Answers to these questions can be formulated, in part, through analysis of public policy conditions that may coalesce to shape financial strategy for community colleges in the late eighties. Following are fourteen conditions that will require the attention of financial administrators between 1985 and 1990:

1. Changing Economic Conditions. The United States economy is undergoing a fundamental restructuring evident in trends such as the transition to a global economy, unusual wage restraints, improving productivity, and the application of sophisticated, labor-saving technology to jobs. Pressing issues remain to be addressed by the Reagan Administration that could adversely impact community college budgets through disruption of the flow of federal revenues to the states. Included among these issues are the federal budget deficit, the import/export imbalance, tax reform, the weakened international competitive position, economic recovery based on total consumption in contrast to corporate investment, and increasing domestic spending requirements. To reduce the budget deficit, the federal government will move to reduce aid and tax benefits to the states using a recently completed Department of Treasury study showing the fiscal condition of the states to be stronger than that of the federal government. Proposals will be made to reduce federal funds for housing, health, and employment programs. The states will be forced to take on greater responsibility for administration of more programs.

In the face of diminished federal aid for domestic programs, new spending requirements for improvement of K–12 education, social services for elderly and economically disadvantaged citizens, road and bridge repairs, modification and expansion of prison facilities, modernization of state hospitals, and expansion of water pollution control facilities over the next five years, what will be the priority of state funding for community college education?

2. Deinstitutionalization of Human Services. Human service organizations will respond to federal cutbacks and rising competition for state funds through deinstitutionalization strategies—the lowering of fixed costs for operations through reduction of the number of clients served. Restrictive admissions and early release programs are deinstitutionalization strategies typically employed by state prisons and hospitals to produce cost savings and evidence of negative impacts associated with a shortfall in operating resources. At issue will be the ability of community colleges to produce evidence of impacts that can compete favorably with those documented by human service organizations in states experiencing resource decline.

3. Centralization of Decision Making in State Agencies. The connection between declining resources, patterns of financial decision making, and public policy are just now beginning to be studied by researchers. The condition of state-level resource austerity induces change in financial decision making in community colleges by affecting the location, number, and distribution of power among actors involved in decisions. In the future, trustees and administrators will experience continued erosion of authority to make financial and programmatic decisions as state agencies, using modern information processing and retrieval technology, expand their control over community college finance. Advanced strategies for centralized decision making will be developed to improve efficiency in the allocation and expenditure of resources. Policy initiatives will be advanced by government officials to reinforce centralized decision making as a method for resource conservation in state and local economies facing cutbacks.

Problems will mount for community college administrators as gatekeepers, queues, and filtered messages are used with increasing regularity by state agencies to control communication. These actions will increase the volume of communications between college administrators and agency officials, thus producing an information overload that will add to the complexity of the job of the financial administrator.

4. Economic Differentiation. A consequence of the changing distribution of population and capital resources among the states will be the differentiation of financial conditions for community college education. As the federal government moves to constrict the flow of revenue and tax benefits to state and local governments, the states will intensify economic development efforts to attract private-sector revenue. Competition will ensue, and federal regulation may be necessary to ensure parity among the states. From the standpoint of public policy, it will be necessary to examine the flow of revenue between the federal government and the states and to determine the types of legislation and spending initiatives that might be adopted by the federal government to improve the economic condition of impoverished states.

Community colleges in states with a recent history of population growth, industrial development, and increased federal spending may experience variation in revenue growth rates as government agencies move to alleviate the disruptive effects of differential growth through equalization of spending. Revenue budgets characterized by double-digit growth in the short term may change to no-growth budgets in the long term as a result of shifts in federal spending priorities. Similarly, colleges in depressed states subjected to a condition of prolonged resource austerity may experience revenue growth as a result of increased domestic spending. Policy initiatives promoted by lawmakers representing the special interests of states experiencing differential economic growth will have an important impact on community college revenue budgets (Alfred, 1983).

5. Future Change in Government Spending Priorities. Recent studies have shown that the percentage of the United States population living at or below the poverty level to be 15.2 percent—the worst since 1964. Studies have also shown that child malnutrition is on the rise in northern industrial cities, in part as a result of federal spending cutbacks in the 1981 Reagan Omnibus Budget Reconciliation Act.

Poverty will become a significant public policy issue in the late eighties. It will become a focus for resource allocation as government agencies target money for special-purpose programs to meet the needs of disenfranchised groups, which, if neglected, could lead to social unrest. At issue will be the capacity of community colleges, through their program/service mix, to take advantage of this shift in spending priorities in the late eighties (United States Conference of Roman Catholic Bishops, 1984).

6. *Changing Focus on Quality.* Changing government spending priorities in the late eighties leading to a renewed focus on domestic issues will alter the focus on quality in community college education. Access will once again become an important issue for two-year colleges to address the changing learning requirements of a population increasingly divided into "haves" and "have-nots" by income, occupational status, and economic mobility. Frustration experienced by disaffected groups holding low-income jobs in a technological economy could result in new or expanded programs for job development, job retraining, and adaptation to technology. Faced with unrest fueled by frustration, federal and state agencies will employ financial incentives to encourage community colleges to relax admissions and retention standards in associate degree programs. Education for low-income and displaced workers will become increasingly important as a method to provide opportunity for expansion of personal income through training in technology. Community colleges with slack in their organizational structure will be able to acquire significant new resources from government agencies in the late eighties if administrators are attuned to public policy issues in a postindustrial economy.

7. *Demographic Transition.* The age distribution and family structure in American society is undergoing change. By 1995, an increasing percentage of citizens will be represented in the fifty-five and older age group compared to their current representation. Concurrent with this trend will be the emergence of the single-parent family as a prominent force in society. Between 1970 and 1980, the number of children from zero to eighteen years of age raised in single-parent families increased from 8.8 million to 12.2 million. In the decade 1980–1990, approximately 50 percent of the children in the zero to eighteen age group will be raised in the single-parent family at some point in this age interval.

While seemingly innocuous as a statistic to community colleges, demographic data of this type have powerful implications for patterns of student choice and federal financial aid policy. Children "rushed through" adolescence by adults seeking to replace a missing partner may attempt to make up for lost years of adolescence through college selection. The residential four-year college affords extensive opportunities for peer interaction. If marketed carefully for appeal to recent high school graduates reared in single-parent families, four-year colleges could increase their market share of high school graduates directly at the expense of community colleges.

8. *Changing Structure of the Labor Market.* The rapid application of technology to the labor market has led to the restructuring of manufacturing, service, and technology industries. Contradictory information is available documenting the growth and decline of these occupational sectors over the next decade. However, assumptions can be made regarding the general direction of growth. Growth is expected in service occupations where a large proportion of the jobs will be located, high-technology occupations in which a small proportion of jobs will be located, and low-technology occupations. Decline is anticipated in the proportion of manufacturing jobs.

For community colleges, change in the structure of the labor market can be either positive or negative depending on the program mix and fixed costs of the institution. Colleges with high fixed costs and a manufacturing-centered program mix in a service region undergoing significant growth in service and high-technology jobs will experience decline in revenues unless significant new resources are found for program development, staff training, and equipment acquisition. What strategies can academic and financial administrators employ to renew academic programs in the context of changing labor market conditions?

9. *Questionable Value of the Associate Degree.* In a labor market marked by changing educational requirements associated with change in technology and the structure of jobs, important questions loom as to the value of the associate degree. Does the degree constitute overeducation for service occupations, with the advantage gained by proprietary institutions offering nonaccredited, short-term courses? Does the degree constitute undereducation for technological occupations, with the advantage gained by universities offering technological courses at the baccalaureate degree level? What is the value of the associate degree in a changing labor market? Can associate degree programs be used to develop generic job skills for application to multiple technologies? Does the future of community colleges in a

changing labor market rest with restructured associate degree programs that successfully merge liberal arts and technical training? Will the direction of the future be realized in course offerings variable in length and location that respond to the short-term training needs of new and displaced workers? What steps will be taken by administrators to restructure the associate degree to preserve institutional vitality in a changing labor market?

10. Divided Public Perceptions of Community College Education. Public opinion polls recently conducted in several states (Michigan, California, and Arizona) reveal positive perceptions of community college education for reasons of low cost, accessibility, and programs relevant to citizen needs (Doucette, 1982; Michigan State Department of Education, 1984). Public understanding of the transfer, occupational, and remedial functions is well established, but confusion reigns with respect to understanding of the community college role beyond these functions. The college is not viewed as the "sole provider" of services for any one educational function, but as one provider in a field of many providers. Public support for community college education expressed in operating dollars may be "soft" when tied to "generalized positive perceptions" of institutional role and "hard" when tied to recognition of "sole provider" status in the delivery of educational services. Viewed in the context of financial management, is it possible that state agencies will place the emphasis on credit-bearing "core" programs in the design of finance formulas? Will they be reluctant to support institutions heavily vested in noncredit programs serving narrowly defined constituencies instead of broad population groups?

11. Incomplete Institutionalization. Questions loom among funding decision makers (state legislatures and coordinating boards) as to the nature and extent of the educational benefits produced by community colleges. Is the college primarily a "centrist" organization providing recognized benefits (for example, degrees, certificates, and transferable credits) to full-time students with traditional educational goals, or is it a "quick-fix" organization serving increasing numbers of part-time students with limited educational goals (job retraining, personal development, cultural enrichment, and so on)? Institutions moving toward complete institutionalization experience a full exchange of resources (money and educational benefits) with funding services; there is little or no confusion about the benefits produced by the college. For state agencies responsible for community college appropriation decisions, institutionalization would be complete when the educational benefits (degrees and certificates) produced by the college approximate a level established through negotiation with agency officials.

12. Loss of Uniqueness. Success in resource procurement leads to emulation and, eventually, to competition among institutions. Community college uniqueness in the form of low student costs, open access, comprehensive program/service mix, and quick response to emerging needs has become a dimension of the past. Nonunionized private colleges and proprietary institutions with simplistic organizational structures can respond quickly to emerging needs. Public four-year colleges can compete effectively with two-year colleges for enrollment through sophisticated technologies. K–12 school districts can offer alternative, low-cost learning paths for adult students through incremental resources available via state agencies. Is it possible that community colleges have achieved a condition of optimum enrollment, and are now on the downward slope of the growth curve?

13. Knowledge and Capital Obsolescence. Rapid advances in technology lead to obsolescence of knowledge among faculty in technical disciplines as well as to obsolescence of equipment in instructional programs. Community college administrators confronted with pressing problems related to changing technical skill requirements in business and industry, aging faculty, and obsolete capital resources face a monumental task of institutional renewal. If two-year college instructional programs are perceived as being marginal in quality due to substandard knowledge and technical skills imparted to students, what will be the impact on financial decisions made by state and federal agencies? Obsolescence of knowledge and capital equipment can become a deterrent to institutional image development with external constituencies in the absence of careful planning by faculty and administrators.

14. Organizational Malaise. Community college faculty and administrators confronted with current problems of optimum enrollment and declining resources could experience malaise if careful efforts are not made toward institutional renewal. A resource-rich institution has unlimited freedom to make decisions about programs and an open growth curve with untapped clienteles. It will function differently than an institution that has the opposite growth profile. The more a community college is in conflict with its major funding sources and the more it depends on them for achievement of its goals, the more resources it will allocate to communicating with these funding sources.

The question to be asked by financial administrators is: What is the impact of organizational malaise on institutional productivity and what adverse public policy initiatives might emerge to improve lagging productivity? In the absence of motivated faculty interested in teaching and learning and of imaginative administrators engaged in novel approaches to problem solving, no community college can hope to influence public policy favorably. The community college that seeks to shape the course of public policy in the future must function as a productive institution capable of eliciting the support and enthusiasm of its members for new and continuing ventures.

Positioning Community Colleges for the Future

What are the implications of these public policy conditions for financial administration in community colleges in the late eighties? Information about policy issues in the external environment applied to the development and control of the operating budget is the process for positioning the college with funding sources and student markets. When information about policy conditions is segmental or inaccurate, the position of the institution with revenue sources and student markets is tempered. Information influences the position of the institution in the quest for students and resources.

Based on the policy issues identified in this chapter, community colleges with a comprehensive program/service mix maintain a number of positioning alternatives that can be implemented to improve resource acquisition in different public policy contexts. The key positioning alternatives are those of: the *centrist* organization, providing an unchanging core of traditional programs and services to a broadly defined population; the *adaptive* organization, providing a changing array of customized programs and services to narrowly defined constituencies; and the *symbiotic* organization providing a carefully defined mix of programs and services in direct cooperation with public- and private-sector organizations in the community.

The centrist organization has the advantage of communicating with a concise institutional image to the public based on commonly understood functions that are the hallmark of community college education. These functions include transfer preparation, occupational education, and remediation. As a positioning alternative, the centrist organization probably functions best in a public policy context marked by relative stability in the labor market, steady economic growth, and constancy in the value of the associate degree. Influence for the centrist organization in resource acquisition is predicated on the ability of faculty and administrators to demonstrate efficient performance in the production of educational benefits (degrees and certificates) that are valued by general segments of the population because of historical prestige assigned to the benefits.

Adaptive organizations are those that function best in a public policy context marked by dynamic change in economic conditions, demographic trends, technology, and social needs. This positioning alternative is predicated on organizational characteristics of flexibility in the decision system, discretionary income for program development, and visionary management focused on strategic planning. Administrators in colleges with these characteristics are able to obtain and manage information about public policy conditions that enable the institution to acquire resources through quick response to emerging needs. Presidents and deans use their knowledge of emerging industry needs and labor market conditions, for example, to develop new courses and curricula, to allocate and reallocate resources, and to develop marketing literature and field contacts to shape the attitudes of key corporate decision makers. The adaptive organization is a constantly changing organization that will acquire resources on the basis of its ability to gauge accurately the direction and velocity of social change.

The symbiotic organization draws power and resources through the relationships it builds with public- and private-sector organizations in the service region. Linkages established with business and industry in the development and marketing of technical programs, placement of graduates, design of facilities, training of faculty, and acquisition of equipment add to the stature of the institution both in the resources it applies to instruction and the image it presents to the community. As a positioning alternative, symbiosis can be applied successfully in a number of different public policy contexts. Its benefits would be most clearly realized, however, in the context of resource scarcity when competitive programs and services offered by four-year colleges blur and diffuse the image presented by community colleges to funding sources and student markets. Using the financial, technical, and political resources of community organizations, two-year colleges can: (1) enhance their appeal to student markets through provision of up-to-date technical programs reflecting a direct linkage of education and work and (2) stabilize or improve the acquisition of revenue from funding sources through political leverage applied to elected officials. Symbiotic relationships help community colleges establish uniqueness and visibility for academic programs. They also provide the college with a channel of influence to policy makers and funding decision makers.

Conclusion

When financial officers have developed the capacity to merge strategic and operational dimensions of financial management, when they apply analytical skills to the interpretation of public policy conditions, and when they understand the linkage between policy conditions and institutional positioning alternatives, there may be little need for application of specialized management systems within the college. Obviously, such an institution is healthy. But under the prevailing conditions of change in the context for public policy and the skill requirements for financial administration, community college leaders should be careful not to confuse institutional survival with health. Professional development of the financial administrator in public policy analysis is a small cost to pay for improved capacity in strategic management.

References

Alfred, R. *Economic Differentiation as a Determinant of Higher Education Pricing and Expenditure Policies and Statewide Public Policy: Implications for Governance.* Washington, D.C.: Association for the Study of Higher Education, 1983.

Doucette, D. S. "Determining Public Priorities for the Support of Community College Missions: A Research Description of the Missions of the Arizona Community Colleges." Paper presented at the annual convention of the American Association of Community and Junior Colleges, St. Louis, Missouri, 1982.

Michigan State Department of Education. *Opinions of Michigan Citizens About Postsecondary Education.* Lansing, Mich.: Project Outreach of Michigan State Board of Education, 1984.

United States Conference of Roman Catholic Bishops. *Pastoral Letter on Catholic Social Teaching and the U.S. Economy.* Draft composed at the United States Conference of Roman Catholic Bishops, Washington, D.C., November 1984.

Richard L. Alfred is associate professor of higher education and director of the community college program at the University of Michigan.

Challenges of rapid technological developments, a
changing economy, increasing competition, and a crisis in
identity are forcing community college leaders to develop
new competencies and adaptive strategies.

Strengthening Financial Management: An Agenda for the Future

Dale F. Campbell

The first two sections of this volume focused on the perceived shift in the role of the community college chief business officer from that of principally budget controller to that of an equal partner in an entrepreneurial team. If such a shift is occurring, not everyone will greet it with enthusiasm. As with any change, many will resist, others will resign or be urged to retire, while others will eagerly learn the new competencies necessary to master their respective roles. In Chapter Nine, Richard L. Alfred called for the professional development of business officials in one such competency—public policy analysis. Professionalizing the management team was found to be one of the successful strategies in turning around declining colleges (Chaffee, 1984). Such initiatives have one primary objective—to improve decision making at the institution. Two principal means are available to achieve this end: (1) leadership development and (2) research. This chapter examines these two means and proposes an agenda for future development to strengthen financial management of the nation's community, technical, and junior colleges.

D. Campbell (Ed.). *Strengthening Financial Management.* New Directions for
Community Colleges, no. 50. San Francisco: Jossey-Bass, June 1985.

Leadership

Challenges of rapid technological developments, a changing economy, increasing competition, and a crisis in identity are forcing community college leaders to develop new competencies and adaptive strategies. The North Carolina Community College Presidents' Leadership Institute, conducted in 1983–84, was designed to help chief executives face these challenges. It focused on the areas of human resource development, resource development and marketing, curriculum structure, and creative leadership and governance. Plans are underway to conduct similar renewal programs designed for middle-level managers (Campbell, 1985). The American Association of Community and Junior Colleges (AACJC) (1985) Public Policy Agenda adopted by the board of directors states that "today community college leaders must be competent in more than one specialty. They must be business officers, academic officers, and planning officers" (p. 50).

Furthering professional development opportunities is one of the goals of the National Council of Community College Business Officials (NCCCBO). NCCCBO has been instrumental in sponsoring programs not only relevant to its membership but also programs that foster the understanding of each faculty and staff member's respective role, responsibilities, and challenges. One such program was titled "How to Phase Out a Program: Implications for Academic and Fiscal Affairs," conducted at the annual AACJC convention where priority was given to institutional teams of chief academic and chief business officers as workshop participants. Similar joint programs will help foster collegiality and the development of institutional entrepreneurial teams.

If entrepreneurial teams are to be effective, consideration should be given to designing special professional development institutes in team building, conflict resolution, goal setting, and so on for the entire top administrative or management council of an institution. Institutional planning retreats can be very effective, where an outside consultant is brought in to lead the planning session. Consider how much more could be gained in carefully planning intense renewal programs with up to six institutions participating in an institute! The Office of Professional Services of the American Association of Community and Junior Colleges is urged to work with the appropriate affiliate councils of the association to develop such a program for its key executive leadership training workshop series.

Dale Parnell (1984), president of AACJC and chief national

spokesperson of the movement, sums up our challenge best in stating that, "if we fail to develop leaders with the competencies to not only see our new frontiers but deal with them effectively, I think we're going to . . . stall in the ability to serve the needs of our citizens as lifelong learners." Opportunities to forge the development of an effective entrepreneurial team merit further planning and field testing.

Research

"Almost every article written on community college research begins with a reference to the fact that there is only limited research available. Once more in this case," states Wattenbarger (1985). "The same may be said: There is some, but not nearly enough, research relating to the mission of the community college and how it is financed" (p.64). In recognition of this fact, the National Council of Community College Business Officials this past year established the NCCCBO Fellow Award to provide financial support for research related to community college finance and administrative services. This volume is in part an effort to establish linkages and build upon the excellent research conducted by the National Center for Higher Education Management Systems (NCHEMS). The Chaffee (1984) study on turnaround strategies for private colleges experiencing decline is an example of this research.

Lawrence (1984) has pointed out that the Chaffee findings may be particularly relevant for community colleges but that they call for further research to validate the results. The Department of Adult and Community College Education (ACCE) at North Carolina State University, headquarters of the National Council of Community College Business Officials, has undertaken a series of research projects related to organizational adaptation. This research builds on the NCHEMS studies to determine their applicability to community colleges.

Additional research is needed on the changing structure, function, and roles of the community college top management team and its chief business officer. Community college organizations have in some instances changed dramatically from the governance patterns Richardson, Blocker, and Bender (1972) first wrote of over a decade ago. Taylor and Anderson (1985), speaking of the recent establishment of development offices in the community colleges, state that these institutional structures are now being patterned more closely after private colleges. To what extent might research on financing private colleges be a window to the future for public community colleges?

Calver's (1984) research on the role and functions of the chief business officer merits extension. Chapter Eleven concludes this volume by examining the apparent emergence in the literature of the entrepreneurial team. To what extent does this exist and how applicable is the shift to other institutions?

The American Association of Community and Junior Colleges is looking to its affiliate councils as one mechanism to identify and research trends and issues and to assist in implementing its public policy initiatives. The AACJC board has asked that the National Council of Community College Business Officials lay the foundation for a position paper on equity in community college funding in state and federal allocations and other programs. As Wattenbarger (1985) stated, it will be crucial to attach any such initiative to college mission.

Alternate Strategies

Even the most successful of entrepreneurs attain a scale of diminishing returns unless the incentive system changes. For example, despite enrollment shifts nationwide to more part-time noncredit continuing education students, funding formulas continue to favor credit curriculum programs. What are the intended and unintended outcomes of these formulas? Leslie (1984) writes of the efforts to respond to the new realities in funding, as does Brinkman's (1984) research at NCHEMS on the effects of the fourth decade of formula budgeting.

NCCCBO is beginning a pilot public policy analysis study to examine the alternate funding measures that states experiencing decline have explored to ensure the quality of their program offerings. The hope is that any resulting models will be tested nationwide in collaboration with other centers for research. These findings should be particularly useful in helping states now experiencing or projecting such declines to improve their decision making.

Much remains to be done as we continue to strive to strengthen the financial management and resulting service to the learners served by the nation's community, technical, and junior colleges.

References

American Association of Community and Junior Colleges. "Public Policy Agenda." *Community and Junior College Journal,* 1985, 55 (5), 48–53.
Brinkman, P. T. "Formula Budgeting: The Fourth Decade." In L. L. Leslie (Ed.),

Responding to New Realities in Funding. New Directions for Institutional Research, no. 43. San Francisco: Jossey-Bass, 1984.

Campbell, D. F. (Ed.). *Leadership Strategies for Community College Effectiveness.* Washington, D.C.: American Association of Community and Junior Colleges, 1985.

Calver, R. A. "The Role and Functions of the Chief Business Officers in Community Colleges." Paper presented at the National Council of Community College Business Officials' conference, Dallas, Texas, November 1, 1984.

Chaffee, E. E. "Successful Strategic Management in Small Private Colleges." *Journal of Higher Education,* 1984, 55 (2), 212–241.

Lawrence, B. "Beyond the Bottom Line." *Community and Junior College Journal,* 1984, 54 (5), 21–23.

Leslie, L. L. (Ed.). *Responding to New Realities in Funding.* New Directions for Institutional Research, no. 43. San Francisco: Jossey-Bass, 1984.

Parnell, D. "Opportunity with Excellence: Vision of the Future." Interview by Dale F. Campbell and Robert M. Stivender, 13 June 1984. Tape recording, American Association of Community and Junior Colleges, Washington, D.C.

Richardson, R. C., Jr., Blocker, C. E., and Bender, L. W. *Governance for the Two-Year College.* Englewood Cliffs, N. J.: Prentice-Hall, 1972.

Taylor, C. A., and Anderson, T. B. "Governance: Structure, Style, and Finance." In D. F. Campbell (Ed.), *Leadership Strategies for Community College Effectiveness.* Washington, D.C.: American Association of Community and Junior Colleges, 1985.

Wattenbarger, J. L. "Community College Mission and Finance." *Community and Junior College Journal,* 1985, 55 (5), 64–65.

Dale F. Campbell is an assistant professor and the coordinator of the community college education program at North Carolina State University, Raleigh, as well as the executive director of the National Council of Community College Business Officials, headquartered at the university.

Materials abstracted from recent additions to the Educational Resources Information Center (ERIC) system provide further information on community college financial management.

Sources and Information: Financial Management at the Community College

Jim Palmer
Diane Zwemer

Until the publication of this sourcebook, college business officials have received very little attention in the community college literature. Of the thousands of documents processed by the ERIC Clearinghouse for Junior Colleges since 1966, fewer than twenty deal directly with these important members of the administrative team.

The fiscal problems of the 1970s and 1980s, however, have prompted many authors to focus their attention on money management, fund raising, financial planning, and other aspects of college administration that campus business officials have quietly handled for years. This chapter—based on a search of ERIC's *Resources in Education* and *Current Index to Journals in Education*—reviews a selection of these writings.

Functions of the Business Officer

LeCroy (1984) is one of the few authors to consider the multifaceted skills needed by today's campus business officer.

D. Campbell (Ed.). *Strengthening Financial Management.* New Directions for Community Colleges, no. 50. San Francisco: Jossey-Bass, June 1985.

Though the talents of these officials are often buried under stereotypic images, LeCroy points out that they must stay in touch with significant educational trends, have the ability to plan, understand the meaning of productivity, and communicate effectively with administrators, faculty, and the public. The need for these skills is borne out by recent documents that examine the problem of financial management at two-year colleges.

Purchasing. The complex nature of college purchasing management is illustrated by Beuhner (1981), who details a study conducted by management at the San Diego Community College District (California) to assess the cost-effectiveness of the reprographic services utilized by district offices. Data were collected to (1) identify the types and quantity of internal reprographic services currently being provided by the district, (2) identify the types of services for which the district was contracting with outside printers, (3) provide an inventory of reprographic equipment in the district, (4) evaluate the cost-effectiveness of reprographic expenditures, and (5) identify more cost-effective alternatives. The study's methodology included interviews with all reproduction supervisors and with various instructors and administrators. In addition, the researchers' reviewed in-house production work, analyzed contracting techniques and costs, and made cost comparisons with other local educational agencies. The study revealed that the district's use of reprographic services was not cost-effective: Machines were not used to full capacity, equipment operators lacked knowledge of effective use of machines, forms were not standardized, and outside vendors were being used when in-house facilities could have been used more cheaply. A reorganization of the dictrict's reprographic services was recommended.

More recently, college managers have focused attention on the purchase and acquisition of computer systems. Miami-Dade Community College (Florida) has established procedures for the purchase of microcomputer programs and equipment to support instructional and administrative functions. The procedures require college departments to justify purchase requests and to verify that there are no alternative methods of performing the functions of the proposed computer or computer system (CAUSE, 1983). Additional information on the planning and procurement of computers and information systems is provided by Conrad and Bender (1983) and by the Virginia State Department of Community Colleges (1981).

Bookstore and Food Service Management. Stumph (1982) reviews factors that college business officers should consider in determining whether the institution should manage its own bookstore and food service operations rather than leasing them to contract operators. While self-operation may provide substantial returns under the right conditions, the author notes that contractors can provide school business officials with professional management, a predictable return, a good cash flow, and escape from accounting, personnel, and management burdens. In addition, contractors enjoy certain advantages over self-operators, including the ability to take advantage of quantity buying, to take risks on impulse merchandise, and to take advantage of new trends in merchandising and administration.

Other authors discussing college retailing operations include Maxon and Bryant (1977), who detail the layout and operation of the bookstore at Prince George's Community College (Maryland); Miller (1982), who reviews the computerized operations at the bookstore at DeAnza Community College (California); and Rushing (1980), who discusses the centralized administration of bookstores at a multicampus college in Texas.

Budgeting. The annual budgeting cycle generates the ebb and flow of the business officers' workload. While accurate budgeting based on timely information is essential to efficient resource allocation and to institutional planning, college business officers are often limited to the budgeting procedures mandated by state authorities.

Elkins (1982) stresses the importance of integrating the planning and budgeting procedures and describes the integration of these two tasks at Cedar Valley College (Texas). The author notes that "the entire budget and planning package is completed and filed by the end of March for the fiscal year beginning the next September 1" (p. 24) and that all units are given a bottom-line budget figure in the preceding fall with which to begin the planning process. The requirements for such a budgeting process include accurate funding projections for the upcoming year, and Elkins maintains that such projections can be derived with a minimum of difficulty from state, local, and federal data sources.

Kozitza (1982) examines budgeting as an allocation problem and details an equity allocation model for multicampus districts and/or large college divisions. Using the model, a study group comprised of representatives from the college and the community first determines the key factors (such as average daily attendance) that affect the need for a specific resource or expenditure object. Then, each of the factors is weighted by individual study group members and the percentage weight of each factor for each expenditure object is averaged. Next, the specific allocation units for each campus or facility are determined and then converted into dollar amounts. Finally, each campus or unit receives a total allocation representing the same total of all expenditure object allocations. Kozitza's model provides for the participation of various college constituencies in the budgeting process. Administrators at other colleges have found such participatory decision making to be politically expedient when budgets are frozen or reduced. (See, for example, Compton Community College, 1981).

Of course, college budgeting is largely governed by state regulations. The Illinois Community College Board (1980) has developed a manual for college business officers that provides a uniform system for accounting, budgeting, auditing, and reporting. Among other things, the manual sets forth definitions for major accounts and funds and specifies the limitations that are imposed on each. In addition, the manual discusses the role and responsibilities of internal auditors as well as mechanisms for internal financial control. Similar accounting guidelines in California are described by the Yosemite Community College District (1983).

State guidelines can simplify the budgeting process, but they sometimes do not meet the budgeting needs of all institutions. A task force in Colorado, for example, found that the state's formula budgeting guidelines did not address adequately the small economies of scale that are characteristic of colleges. The task force recommended several formula changes (Colorado State Board for Community Colleges and Occupational Education, 1978).

Managing Retrenchment

The business officer's mettle is put to a severe test when he or she manages retrenchment rather than growth. In hard economic times, the business officer needs more than bookkeeping skills; she or he needs to work with administration in developing a strong college identity, setting priorities on the basis of that identity, allocating resources on the basis of those priorities, and communicating the benefits of the institution to the public and to funding agencies (Lawrence, 1984). Several documents illustrate the complex nature of the retrenchment problem.

Sheldon (1983) maintains that reduced funding necessarily forces college managers to make decisions regarding which courses and programs to eliminate, which students to disenfranchise educationally, and the priorities that should be assigned to courses. Thus, managing retrenchment is largely a matter of information gathering and assessment; data are needed on the relative value of courses or programs to the community, the costs of these courses and programs, and the availability of similar instruction elsewhere in the community. Sheldon stresses that decisions about which courses and programs to cut should be made with the aid of those who are best positioned to make those decisions—that is, the faculty, administrators, and trustees of individual colleges, rather than state-level administrators.

Lowe (1983) describes the operation of this decision-making process at Foothill College (California). For each institutional program, criteria for determining effectiveness, revenue efficiency, and centrality to the college mission are specified and weighted. An evaluation committee is formed and programs are selected for review. Data are collected, a quartile score is assigned by the committee for each criterion, and scores are multiplied by the weight factor assigned for each criterion. During 1981–82, when the college experienced severe budget cuts, six of the ten lowest-ranked programs were eliminated from the college's curriculum.

It is easy to see, then, that business officers and other financial managers at the college need to understand the integration of educational planning and institutional budgeting. Casey (1982) emphasizes that allocation decisions made in the face of budget cuts can drastically alter the course of a college. Depending on the severity of the cuts, management responses can be as mild as a slight reduction of services on a proportional basis across programs or as harsh as cutbacks in whole categories of programs and, concomitantly, the reformulation of the college mission. Additional information on procedures used to manage retrenchment at the institutional level are provided by Clagett (1981), Murphy (1983), and Nichols and Stewart (1983).

Private Financial Support

In response to fiscal exigency, many two-year institutions have established college development offices and have begun to augment budgets with private donations. Wattenbarger (1975) argues that the responsibilities of the college development officer require that he or she have more than a knowledge of fund-raising techniques; resources must be developed with college goals in mind, and the development officer must be a professional educator with an understanding of the total college program. Behrendt (1984) maintains that fund raising should be the responsibility of none other than the college president. The president, Behrendt argues, should establish and maintain ties with potential donors; the college development officer, on the other hand, should act as a logistical person who arranges meetings and manages the paperwork of direct mailing, deferred giving, and other technical aspects of the fund-raising effort. Fund raising is no longer an auxiliary management task.

Seeking the Support of Alumni. As community colleges become older and their graduates more numerous, alumni associations are taking on larger roles in institutional support. These organizations, discussed by Kopecek (1980) and by McCracken and others (1980), are valuable sources of alternative funds and can aid the college in developing political support, fostering positive public opinion toward the college, recruiting new students, and locating potential donors. The authors mentioned above discuss several factors that should be considered when organizing an office of alumni affairs. First, community college students don't often identify with a particular class year. Therefore, it may be necessary to form special-interest groups for alumni of individual vocational programs or for alumni who, while students, participated in college theater, athletics, or student government. Second, each college needs to determine who is an alumnus; one college, for example, defined an alumnus as anyone who had completed four or more courses. Third, the college should assign a staff person to alumni affairs, make funds available, and establish an alumni newsletter. Finally, these efforts should be undertaken with the realization that success depends on the degree to which the alumni association serves the interest of its members. While soliciting the support of alumni, for example, colleges should provide former students with opportunities for involvement in campus activities and offer continual services in the areas of placement, lifelong learning, and job retraining.

Corporate Funding. Corporate funding has become an important resource for many colleges. Milligan (1982), for example, describes the success of Monroe Community College (New York) in seeking financial support from local industries that benefit from the college's vocational programs. Most of the college's efforts involved the solicitation of funds for specific purposes such as special programs, equipment, training activities, or financial aid for students. Milligan notes that most fund raising in the past has arisen from spontaneous, unplanned contact with the business world. The fund-raising program at Monroe Community College, on the other hand, represents a relatively new attempt at planned solicitation of corporate donations. Additional information on corporate support is provided by Ballard (1981), who describes the success of Delta College

(Mississippi) in attracting the attention and support of local corporations through the college's radio station.

College Foundations. Some community colleges have established foundations that promote and facilitate corporate, alumni, and other private funding. Kopecek (1982–1983) points out that a foundation "is incorporated under appropriate state law in such a manner as to qualify for federal tax-exempt status" (p. 12). Thus, donations to the foundation are tax deductible, while donations to the public college are not. Monies donated to the foundation can go toward special scholarships, sophisticated equipment, daycare centers for students' children, and other projects not provided for in the public budget.

Steps in the development of a foundation are described by Olivanti (1983) in his discussion of the foundation at Michigan's Kalamazoo Valley Community College (KVCC). The college first had its attorney draw up articles of incorporation and bylaws. Subsequent steps included (1) securing tax-exempt status for the foundation, (2) securing a charitable solicitation license from the Michigan State Attorney General, (3) putting together information for prospective donors, (4) involving trustees in selecting foundation board members, and (5) determining a fund-raising strategy. KVCC determined that deferred giving, rather than solicitation of small cash donations, would be the major emphasis of its fund-raising strategy.

Of course, steps in the development of a foundation will vary from state to state. But the rewards can be great. Olivanti notes that KVCC used the fund generated by its foundation to develop community services and continuing education activities. These areas had been particularly hard hit by cuts in public support. Additional information on community college foundations is provided by Davidson and Wise (1982), who discuss the role of foundations and other fund-raising tactics in college institutional development, and by Duffy (1980), who examines the characteristics of successful foundations.

Revenue Diversification. One approach to alternative funding is revenue diversification. This approach, discussed by Brightman (1982) and Scigliano (1980), involves the college in commercial activities that are undertaken specifically to support educational programs and services. Such for-profit ventures include food catering, retailing (at the bookstore, for example), leasing campus facilities, and granting concessions. Brightman stresses that colleges seeking to diversify revenue sources should (1) take advantage of the physical assets they possess, (2) identify different areas of retail sales on campus (bookstore, photocopy machines, and so on), (3) recruit experts to advise on legal and business matters, (4) engage the help of small-business associations, (5) obtain approval from the board of trustees, and (6) establish a committee to oversee the diversification effort.

Both Brightman and Scigliano focus on problems that need to be overcome in pursuing a revenue diversification plan. Foremost of these are the perceptions that for-profit ventures are inappropriate, that most of the money gained will be lost in taxes, and that attention to revenue diversification matters will dilute the college's mission. The legitimacy of such ventures is assured, Scigliano maintains, as long as they are approved by the board of trustees and "are consistent with the basic educational mission of the college—either tied to a program interest (technology or business), a function (library), or a need for a service (cafeteria or bookstore)" (p. 10).

Grantsmanship. Rude (1979) points out that community colleges take in disproportionately small percentages of the grant money awarded to institutions of higher education. This problem, he argues, is largely due to the fact that community college faculty, unlike their colleagues at four-year colleges and universities, are not provided with incentives to initiate and fund individual research projects. Community college professionals, then, are just beginning to learn about the grantsmanship process.

To facilitate this learning, Hellweg (1980) urges each community college to establish its own grants office. The office should: (1) maintain a library of periodicals and other materials on funding agencies and proposal preparation; (2) develop a campus "fundability" profile that identifies grants for which the college and individual instructors can apply; (3) assist faculty in the proposal development process; and (4) maintain a liaison between the college and funding agencies. Bartkovich (1981) describes how college library personnel can assist the grantsmanship center by providing faculty and staff with instruction on the identification and use of reference materials that provide information on funding sources.

Planning the Future

As Alfred points out in Chapter Nine, college financial managers need to shift their attention from day-to-day operations to strategic planning. The importance of a future-oriented approach to financial management is underscored by the large number of authors who have examined strategic planning at the community college. In an earlier volume in the *New Directions for Community Colleges* series, Palmer (1983) reviewed forty-seven documents on strategic planning that were entered into the ERIC data base in the early 1980s. Additional articles in that *New Directions* volume discuss the components and methods of strategic management (Myran, 1983); the effect of external agencies, businesses, and associations on the college's future (Gollattscheck, 1983); the strategic elements of an instutional plan (Groff, 1983); the signs of organizational growth and maturity (Lorenzo, 1983); and the role of the chief executive officer in strategic staff development (Armes and O'Banion, 1983).

Recent Literature on Strategic Management. Since the publication of the above-mentioned *New Directions* volume, several documents have been added to the ERIC collection on strategic management. In the most comprehensive of these documents, Martens (1982) provides a framework for determining whether the planning and control systems used by New York community colleges could be made more effective by applying management technologies used in the private sector. She reviews and compares the state of the art in strategic planning at profit-making business organizations, nonprofit organizations, community colleges, and other institutions of higher education. Based on this analysis and on a review of laws and regulations governing the use of stragetic planning and management control in the New York community colleges, she concludes with tentative recommendations for planning reform.

Models of strategic planning in California are presented in a document published jointly by the California Community Colleges, the Western Association of Schools and Colleges, and the Accrediting Commission for Community and Junior Colleges (*Models of Strategic Planning . . .*, 1983). The document first provides an overview of current challenges to academic management and strategic planning and then describes the strategic planning projects at four California community colleges or districts: San Francisco Community College District, Long Beach City College, Riverside City College, and the Yosemite Community College District. Each case report presents a brief characterization of the planning project; information on organizational structures, premises, assumptions, and procedures; a history of the project; and a general commentary. The monograph concludes with a discussion of the unique and common characteristics of the projects.

Using Planning Data. How do colleges organize and use the information gathered in strategic planning? Several documents synthesize planning data and discuss their implications. Bannister and Greenhill (1983), for example, marshal socioeconomic data collected by the British Columbia Institute of Technology (BCIT) to draw conclusions regarding the demand for postsecondary education in the institute's service district, the future demand for BCIT graduates in the labor market, the curricular changes that will be needed in response to advancing technology in the workplace, and the need for new sources of funding in the wake of fiscal cutbacks. In another analysis, Coffey (1984) examines how the California community colleges, and the Los Rios Community College District in particular, are affected by such external forces as the aging population, high minority enrollments, limits on governmental spending, state regulations, the trend toward centralization, and enrollment-driven funding formulas. Similar studies of the impact of socioeconomic and political changes on colleges are presented by Donnelly and others (1983), who present a master plan for Central Ohio Technical College; by Fisher (1984), who speculates on the future of Modesto Junior College (California); by Gonzales and Keyser (1984), who describe strategic planning at Linn-Benton Community College (Oregon); and by the Alamo Community College District (1983), which analyzes the challenges that will confront the district in the areas of curricular change, financial support, and space and facilities planning.

These and other documents on strategic planning underscore the complexity of the tasks faced by today's college managers. As Ellison (1982) points out, strategic management involves the generation and implementation of strategies for the investment of institutional resources in activities aimed at promoting organizational growth. Its basic elements include environmental analysis and forecast of conditions relevant to the institution; an internal resource audit; and the formulation, solution, and implementation of strategies and objectives. Since planning and budgeting are so tightly interwoven in this strategic management process, the college business office is a key member of the institution's administrative team.

Where to Find Items in the Reference List

The items listed in the following section represent a sample of the documents and journal articles in the ERIC data base that examine community college governance. The items marked with an "ED" number can be ordered through the ERIC Document Reproduction Service (EDRS) in Alexandria, Virginia, or obtained on microfiche at over 650 libraries across the country. Items not marked with an "ED" number are journal articles; they are not available on microfiche or through EDRS and must be obtained through regular library channels. For an EDRS order form and/or a list of the libraries in your state that have ERIC microfiche collections, please contact the ERIC Clearinghouse for Junior Colleges, 8118 Math-Sciences Building, UCLA, Los Angeles, California 90024.

References

Alamo Community College District. *Strategic Issues: Priorities for the Future.* San Antonio, Tex.: Alamo Community College District, 1983. 16 pp. (ED 231 424)

Armes, N., and O'Banion, T. "The Role of the Chief Executive Officer in Strategic Staff Development." In G. A. Myran (Ed.), *Strategic Management in the Community College.* New Directions for Community Colleges, no. 44. San Francisco: Jossey-Bass, 1983. (ED 238 477)

Ballard, W. J. "It's All in the Community: Community Colleges Can Win Corporate Support." *CASE Currents,* 1981, *7* (10), 42–43.

Bannister, D., and Greenhill, C. *1983 Outlook Report.* Burnaby: British Columbia Institute of Technology, Office of Institutional Planning, 1983. 146 pp. (ED 245 727)

Bartkovich, J. P. *Library Reference and the Grantsmanship Process.* Unpublished report, 1981. 19 pp. (ED 208 893)

Behrendt, R. L. "Honors Programs and Private Funding: How One Community College Succeeded." Paper presented at the annual convention of the American Association of Community and Junior Colleges, Washington, D.C., April 1984. 15 pp. (ED 244 682)

Beuhner, S. *San Diego Community College District Reprographic Services Study.* San Diego: San Diego Community College District, 1981. 42 pp. (ED 211 131)

Brightman, R. W. "Revenue Diversification: A New Source for Community Colleges." Unpublished paper, 1982. 24 pp. (ED 221 251)

Casey, J. W. *Managing Contraction: An Institution Experiences Contraction—Seattle Community College District, Seattle, Washington, U.S.A.* Seattle: Seattle Community College District, 1982. 17 pp. (ED 229 064)

CAUSE. "Micros on Campus: Policy Issues. Current Issues Forum." In CAUSE, *Information Resources and the Individual—Proceedings of the CAUSE National Conference (San Francisco, California, December 11–14, 1983).* Boulder, Colo.: CAUSE, 1983. 525 pp. (ED 244 542)

Clagett, C. A. *Community College Policies for the Coming Financial Squeeze. Working Paper no. 4.* Largo, Md.: Prince George's Community College, 1981. 41 pp. (ED 205 245)

Coffey, J. C. *Planning for Change: Assessing Internal and External Environmental Factors.* Sacramento, Calif.: Los Rios Community College District, 1984. 205 pp. (ED 243 530)

Colorado State Board for Community Colleges and Occupational Education. *Small College Budgeting: A Funding Proposal Prepared by and for Colorado's Small Public Colleges—Analyst's Technical Report.* Denver: Colorado State Board for Community Colleges and Occupational Education, 1978. 47 pp. (ED 213 459)

Compton Community College. *The Financial Resource Allocation Process at Compton Community College: A Redirection.* Compton, Calif.: Compton Community College Federation of Teachers, 1981. 41 pp. (ED 229 055)

Conrad, L. P. and Bender, L. W. *Computers and Information Systems in the Small Two-Year*

128

College. Tallahassee: Florida State University, Institute for Studies in Higher Education, 1983. 86 pp. (ED 225 637)

Davidson, M. M., and Wise, S. R. "Fund Raising—The Public Two-Year College." In P. S. Bryant and J. A. Johnson (Eds.), *Advancing the Two-Year College.* New Directions for Institutional Advancement, no. 15. San Francisco: Jossey-Bass, 1982.

Donnelly, B. L., and others. *Central Ohio Technical College Annual Plan, 1983–84: Academic Affairs.* Newark: Central Ohio Technical College, 1983. 91 pp. (ED 241 082)

Duffy, E. H. *Characteristics and Conditions of a Successful Community College Foundation.* Resource Paper no. 23. Washington, D.C.: National Council for Resource Development, 1980. 13 pp. (ED 203 918)

Elkins, F. "Integrate Budgeting with Planning." *American School and University,* 1982, 55 (3), 24.

Ellison, N. M. "Managing and Financing Urban Community Colleges in the Eighties: The Case for Strategic Management." Paper presented at the National Urban Community College conference, Detroit, Mich., March 1982. 21 pp. (ED 223 286)

Fisher, P. *MJC: Planning for the Future—An Assessment of the External Environment: Identifying Problems, Constraints, and Opportunities.* 1st ed. Modesto, Calif.: Modesto Junior College, 1984, 93 pp. (ED 245 730)

Gollattscheck, J. F. "Strategic Elements of External Relationships." In G. A. Myran (Ed.), *Strategic Management in the Community College.* New Directions for Community Colleges, no. 44. San Francisco: Jossey-Bass, 1983. (ED 238 477)

Gonzales, T., and Keyser, J. *Strategic Planning for Linn-Benton Community College: President's Perspective.* Albany, Or.: Linn-Benton Community College, 1984. 34 pp. (ED 244 679)

Groff, W. H. "Strategic Planning." In G. A. Myran (Ed.), *Strategic Management in the Community College.* New Directions for Community Colleges, no. 44. San Francisco: Jossey-Bass, 1983. (ED 238 477)

Hellweg, S. A. "Requisites for an Effective College Grants Development Operation." *Community College Review,* 1980, *8* (2), 5–12.

Illinois Community College Board. *Illinois Community College Board Uniform Accounting Procedures Manual.* Springfield: Illinois Community College Board, 1980. 142 pp. (ED 219 091)

Kopecek, R. J. "The Alumni—An Untapped Reservoir of Support." Paper presented at the "Creating New Markets" conference of the National Council on Community Services and Continuing Education, Danvers, Mass., October 1980. 17 pp. (ED 195 317)

Kopecek, R. J. "An Idea Whose Time Is Come: Not-For-Profit Foundations for Public Community Colleges." *Community College Review,* 1982–1983, *10* (3), 12–17.

Kozitza, G. A. *Equity Allocation Model for Multicampus Districts and/or Large Divisions.* Ventura, Calif.: Ventura County Community College District, 1982. 21 pp. (ED 225 614)

Lawrence, B. "Beyond the Bottom Line: Good Managers Look to Results." *Community and Junior College Journal,* 1984, *54* (5), 21–23.

LeCroy, R. J. "Business Officials Share Buried Talents." *Community and Junior College Journal,* 1984, *54* (5), 37–39.

Lorenzo, A. L. "Strategic Elements of Financial Management." In G. A. Myran (Ed.), *Strategic Management in the Community College.* New Directions for Community Colleges, no. 44. San Francisco: Jossey-Bass, 1983. (ED 238 477)

Lowe, I. D. *Program Evaluation at Foothill College.* Los Altos, Calif.: Foothill College, 1983. 30 pp. (ED 231 406)

Martens, F. R. H. *Community College Strategic Planning and Management Control Reform in New York State: An Issue Paper.* Poughkeepsie, N.Y.: Dutchess Community College, 1982. 159 pp. (ED 238 507)

Maxon, H. C., and Bryant, M. "Prince George's Community College Bookstore in Largo." *College Store Journal,* 1977, *44* (4), 116–121.

McCracken, J. E. and others. "Community/Junior College Alumni: Initiative, Influence, and Impact—A National Forum." Papers presented at the annual convention of the American Association of Community and Junior Colleges, San Francisco, March 30–April 2, 1980. 11 pp. (ED 190 171)

Miller, C. "Who Can Afford a Computerized Bookstore? Almost Anyone." *College Store Journal,* 1982, *49* (6), 76–78.

Milligan, F. G. "Corporate Solicitation, SUNY Style: A Two-Year Urban Campus's Approach to Corporate Giving " Paper presented at the State University of New York's (SUNY's) conference. "A Perspective on Corporate Giving," Corning, N.Y., November 9, 1982. 13 pp. (ED 225 625)

Models of Strategic Planning in Community Colleges. Sacramento: California Community Colleges, Office of the Chancellor; Aptos, Calif.: Western Association of Schools and Colleges, Accrediting Commission for Community and Junior Colleges, 1983. 70 pp. (ED 242 360)

Murphy, M. T. *Policies and Procedures Relating to Program Redirection and Financial Exigency.* Bel Air, Md.: Harford Community College, 1983. 16 pp. (ED 227 910)

Myran, G. A. "Strategic Management in the Community College." In G. A. Myran (Ed.), *Strategic Management in the Community College.* New Directions for Community Colleges, no. 44. San Francisco: Jossey-Bass, 1983. (ED 238 477)

Nichols, D. D., and Stuart, W. H. *In Praise of Fewer Administrators.* Washington, D.C.: American Association of Community and Junior Colleges, 1983. 26 pp. (ED 227 889)

Olivanti, R. A. "Founding a College Foundation: A Mini Case Study." *Community Services Catalyst,* 1983, *8* (2), 14–16.

Palmer, J. "Sources and Information: Strategic Management." In G. A. Myran (Ed.), *Strategic Management in the Community College.* New Directions for Community Colleges, no. 44. San Francisco: Jossey-Bass, 1983. (ED 238 477)

Rude, J. C. "Special Concerns of Two-Year Colleges." In K. Mohrman (Ed.), *Grants: View from the Campus.* Washington, D.C.: Association of American Colleges, 1979. 88 pp. (ED 201 239)

Rushing, J. B. "Managing the Multicampus—Twelve Years Later." *Community and Junior College Journal,* 1980, *50* (6), 16–20.

Scigliano, J. A. "Strategic Marketing Planning: Creative Strategies for Developing Unique Income Sources." Paper presented at the annual conference of the National Council on Community Services and Continuing Education, Danvers, Mass., October 1980. 22 pp. (ED 196 474)

Sheldon, M. S. *Research and Educational Decisions: An Editorial.* Unpublished paper, 1983. 10 pp. (ED 230 217)

Stumph, W. J. "In-House Versus Franchise College Food Services and Bookstores." Paper presented at the conference of the Association of School Business Officials, Atlanta, Georgia, November 1982. 7 pp. (ED 225 628)

Virginia State Department of Community Colleges. *Master Plan for the Virginia Community College System Computing Services.* Richmond: Virginia State Department of Community Colleges, 1981. 198 pp. (ED 241 088)

Wattenbarger, J. L. "The Role of the Professional Educator as the College Development Officer." Resource Paper no. 7. Paper presented at the annual meeting of the Florida Council for Resource Development, Washington, D.C., April 1975. 11 pp. (ED 203 919)

Yosemite Community College District. *Assessment Guide.* Modesto, Calif.: Yosemite Community College District, 1983. 76 pp. (ED 246 950)

Jim Palmer is assistant director for user services at the ERIC Clearinghouse for Junior Colleges, University of California, Los Angeles.

Diane Zwemer is user services librarian at the ERIC Clearinghouse for Junior Colleges, University of California, Los Angeles.

Index

131